KEEP IT SIMPLE

KEEP IT SIMPLE: DIET AND EXERCISE

Seven Simple Tips for a Healthy, Active Lifestyle

〜〜〜

Luigi Gratton, MD

Library of Congress CIP data applied for.

Copyright © 2008 by Luigi Gratton, MD. All rights reserved.
Printed in the United States of America. Except as permitted under
the United States Copyright Act of 1976, no part of this publication
may be reproduced or distributed in any form or by any means, or
stored in a database or retrieval system, without the prior written
permission of the publisher.

1 2 3 4 5 6 7 8 9 0/0 9 8 7 6 5 4 3 2 1

ISBN 10/ 0-9801711-0-5.
        13/978-0-9801711-0-5

Interior design and production: Robert S. Tinnon Design

Cover design by: Mint Reaction

Photography by: Micah Smith

To order additional copies of this book visit our Web site:

www.drluigi.com

TO MY MOM AND DAD

CONTENTS

ACKNOWLEDGMENTS

Family
My Mom, Ponsella, My Dad, Rudy, My Brother, Luca,
My Sister, Janet, My Nieces, Petrina and Giovanna

Friends
William Turner MD, Luis Moreno, MD, Jeremy Williams, MD,
Billy Brown, Stacy Payne,
and last, but certainly not least, Patricia Manzo

Support
Sonal Sahay, Robert Tinnon, Rena Copperman,
Kashi Copperman, Lori Collins, and Micah Smith

Mentors
David Heber, MD, Michael O. Johnson, Steve Henig PhD,
Susan Bowerman, RD, and Jack Kavulich.

INTRODUCTION

For the first time in our history, we have a health crisis with obesity. Never before, in any civilization past, have we seen so many people overweight and obese. The problem is getting worse, every day, in every country. It's no mystery why the world is suffering from this challenge. Globally, societies are consuming far more calories than they need while performing far too little physical activity. It's a simple balancing act of how many calories we eat and how much energy we expend. But the scale is being tipped far too much on the calorie side. It may not seem like a serious problem. But the consequences of weight gain are very serious. Every day, health care practitioners are treating obesity-related conditions throughout the world, so-called *chronic diseases* and *lifestyle diseases*. The point is that these conditions are quite preventable with good nutrition and physical activity.

The most recent data on the prevalence of either overweight or obese individuals is incredible. For the first time there are more people overweight than underweight. Anthropologists have strong evidence of our existence from tens to hundreds of thousands of years past. Based on human remains, scientists have been able to understand the body sizes and shapes of our ancestors. We know that we've never before had obese societies. In civilizations past, we've never had an abundance in the food supply as we do today. Nature prepared us well for food scarcity. Humans have adapted to survival with minimal food calories. But Mother Nature never predicted technological advances in the food supply. Humans are simply not well prepared for the overabundance of food that we have today. This excessive supply of calories is everywhere: developed and underdeveloped nations, rich and poor societies.

Obesity does not discriminate. People of all races, colors, and religions are facing this challenge.

How do we know how widespread these conditions are? The data speaks for itself. There are many organizations that record data related to health care. One of the largest is the World Health Organization (WHO), which regularly publishes data on various health conditions. The most recent data report 850 million people as underweight, while a staggering 1.6 billion people are overweight.

Consider these numbers for a moment.

- Worldwide, there are almost twice as many people overweight than underweight. There are specific countries that have much higher prevalence rates than others. But even those countries considered "healthy" are feeling the effects of the modern diet and lifestyle. The United States has long been considered a center of innovation and technology. Fast food was created in the western United States. So it's no surprise that the United States is leading the charge with well over 65 percent of the population being at least overweight, and a significant percentage being obese. These are frightening numbers when you consider that the United States has over 300 million people.
- Although the United States is currently the global leader in overweight and obese population, other countries, such as Mexico and Brazil, are recording record high prevalence rates of obesity. Countries that have long been considered places for a healthy diet and lifestyle are now facing similar

challenges. Both China and India are experiencing rapid economic growth. With this rapid economic growth come changes in the diet and lifestyle. Both China and India have over one billion people each, and the fast-food companies are expanding in both countries. With more time spent on computers and phones and less on physical activity, we've only begun to see the problem.

Many health educators see the impending storm on the horizon. Every single day, the prevalence rates continue to increase. Many specialists in the field of nutrition speak of a "tsunami" of nutritionally related diseases coming to every developed nation. If societies do not respond to this problem, we will have a global health crisis. The problem is not the extra weight that many humans carry around; the problem is the associated disease that comes with the extra weight. Doctors have never experienced this in medicine. Every aspect of medicine is affected, including pediatrics, internal medicine, obstetrics and gynecology, surgery, and psychiatry. The problem is already here, and it's getting worse every day. To soften the blow of an impending worldwide pandemic, we as health care advocates must take some basic steps in the right direction. We already have the most advanced medicine available, but this is doing little to nothing with the worldwide phenomenon.

Raising awareness is the key. We as a global society are in dire need of increased education on nutrition.

So let's keep it simple. We know the problem—too many empty calories in the diet and too little physical activity. That's evident, we can all agree on that. But what's the solution? What diet is the right diet? What type of exercise is correct?

Everyone has heard the doctor say the words *diet* and *exercise*. But often the doctor that is saying it doesn't know anything about either of these areas. Unfortunately, physicians are not trained in nutrition or exercise in medical school. So most physicians are seeing patients with nutritionally related diseases but do not have the tools to help them.

So many diet and exercise books confuse people with special programs with advanced scientific rationale when the real problem comes down to two areas: diet and exercise. These are the two main topics of discussion in *Keep it Simple*.

I have taken a very simple approach in this book. Half of *Keep it Simple* focuses on diet, the other half on exercise. Nothing complicated, just a commonsense approach backed by good science.

PART ONE

DIET

CUT CALORIES, NOT FOOD

I n any country, on any food label, you will notice nutritional information, based on a diet of around 2,000 calories per day. This is the basis for first Simple Diet Tip.

READ YOUR FOOD LABELS

There is a good reason why every food label in the world lists 2,000 as the average daily caloric intake. It's because the average person needs approximately 2,000 calories per day to live. Some require a little less, some a little more. These differences depend largely on body size. For example, a seventy-five-year-old woman of petite stature and minimal muscle mass may only need 1,100 calories a day to perform her daily routine. Meanwhile, on the other side of the spectrum, a young professional football player may require well over 6,000 calories a day to perform. There will always be a broad range that makes us unique as humans; we come in all shapes and sizes. So the older woman and the young football player serve as examples to illustrate the opposite ends of the spectrum. The average person will fall somewhere in between these two examples, and for the average person, the 2,000-calorie/day average is just about right.

This physiological fact is very important to understand as it sets the stage for both diet and exercise each day.

When counseling patients in the clinic, I generally try to target their daily caloric intake to somewhere in the neighborhood of 1,500 calories because most people can consume sufficient nutrients in the diet and keep the calories below 2,000, thus getting weight-management results.

Understanding that the average person needs around 2,000 daily calories is even more important when we consider that we are eating far in excess of those calories. There must be a reason that every day the world has more obese people in it than the previous day. And the reason is that we are eating more and more calories every day. Most experts in the field of nutrition agree that we are eating well over 3,000 calories per day. This may appear to be a shocking piece of evidence, but it helps to explain why the world is getting bigger every single day on the typical Western diet.

FAST FOOD: THE PATH OF LEAST RESISTANCE

So the fact of the matter is, I always recommend you strive to eat as natural and as healthy as possible. The problem is that in today's society, it's very challenging to maintain a healthy diet.

An increasing number of us are leading hectic lives with less time spent preparing fresh food. Both single- and multiple-parent households are working longer hours with less time spent with their families. In a time in which business demands increased productivity, the average worker is putting in more hours at work, meaning that they have fewer hours outside of work. Fewer hours outside of work means fewer hours picking fresh food from the garden, shopping for fresh food, and of course preparing fresh food. Fast food is cheap, easy, and quick. It's what I call the path of least resistance. It fits into the modern family lifestyle all too well. Parents can save money and time buying it and kids are all too often asking for it given the widespread advertising that targets the youth. With powerful ad campaigns generated by the fast-food companies, children become easy targets for poor nutrition. Once the kids are swayed through advertising, they continually make requests to their parents for visits to their favorite fast-food stop. A quick drive through and a pickup of "value packs" for the family and before you know it, the cycle has started. The interesting thing is that often it has little to do with food; often it's the associated toy or movie that brings them in, and the hamburger and soda that bring them back.

As I travel worldwide, I am continually amazed at the penetration of fast food into the family structure. It's truly incredible to see the number of new fast-food restaurants that continue to grow. Even in the most traditional of Eastern cultures, there is a rapid acceptance of the Western diet. As traditional lifestyles become modernized, so do the dietary practices. Fast-food restaurants are growing at a rapid rate, and they are gradually penetrating all cultures around the world.

My mother and father raised me on fresh food. The only thing in our freezer was ice and ice cream. I never knew about microwave meals and frozen snacks. By the time I was old enough to choose my own foods, fast food was a novelty for me. My taste buds were accustomed to foods that were prepared fresh every day. Children who start eating a healthful diet when they are young tend to continue eating a healthful diet as they grow up.

Children develop their taste for certain foods early on. If they start life eating fast foods, they tend to have a poor dietary prognosis, meaning their diets generally stay the same or get worse. If children eat good foods early on, it sets the tone for good nutrition later on in life.

This was certainly the case with me. But many children I went to school with had only prepacked food or even worse, their parents would pack them nothing and drop off fast food at lunchtime. Currently, there are various public health campaigns that focus on children's dietary habits. The sooner that we can promote healthful eating in kids, the better. Although I am a critic of fast food, I must admit that I've certainly had my share of fast food in the past. I have never met anyone who has not eaten fast food. The availability and variety is astounding, and the frequency at which people are now consuming fast food has increased significantly. This is one of the many reasons the rate of obesity is growing every day worldwide.

CALORIES

Calories come in different forms, both solids and liquids. The solids are obviously the hamburgers, fries, hot dogs, pizza, tacos, cookies, cakes, and other foods that are known to be high in calorie but low in nutrients. However the liquid calories are often overlooked. They include sodas, coffees, ice cream shakes, energy drinks, hydration drinks, teas, alcoholic beverages, fruit juices, smoothies, and instant breakfast drinks. These are often packed with sugar calories and are low in essential nutrients. Generally, the food companies do not fortify these types of drinks with important vitamins or minerals. These drinks are usually pleasing to the taste and inexpensive. High-calorie sodas are a major part of this equation, which I discuss in the next chapter along with other high-calorie liquids that have gained popularity in recent years. Recently there has been an explosion in the number of coffeehouses around the world. Caffeine itself does not pose a danger to health; it is the associated sugars that are often hidden in many of these popular drinks that are adding to the

problem. Another explosion has been seen in the mass marketing of energy drinks that are generally heavily caffeinated, filled
with sweeteners, and light on nutrients. The marketing push has
been toward health and vitality, but most of the major energy
drinks are void of nutrition. They mainly function as stimulants
from the caffeine and sugar.

Calories are currently the main problem and will continue to
be until we become better educated on nutrition. So remember:
the predominant issue with this pandemic of overweight and obesity is calories. Although the average consumer is ignorant of
daily caloric requirements, simple steps must be taken to become
more aware on this issue.

NUTRIENT DENSITY

Cutting calories, not food simply means eating foods that are
"nutrient dense," that is, packed with good things. Often foods
that are nutrient dense, such as vegetables, are low in calories.
Vegetables are one of the best examples of nutrient density. They
have very few calories per serving and are packed with vitamins,
minerals, antioxidants, and fiber. These are the foods our ancestors consumed, the foods that Mother Nature intended for us
to eat.

On the opposite side of the spectrum are nutrient-poor foods
that are "calorically dense," that is, high in calories but very low
in nutrients. The vast majority of these foods are manmade. A
great example is soda. The typical regular soda has a tremendous
amount of sugar without any nutritional value in it. Diet sodas
limit the sugar with the addition of artificial sweeteners, but they
are also void of nutrients. Nutrient-poor, high-calorie foods are
becoming typical parts of the modern diet: hamburgers, french
fries, pizza, tacos, hotdogs, potato chips, candies, fried chicken,

and so forth. Anything that ancient woman and man did not eat 10,000 years ago is artificial and therefore generally high in calories and low in nutrients.

Whatever you call it—engineered food, fast food, packaged food, processed food—it's all engineered. As more societies move toward a Western lifestyle, more people are consuming these manmade foods. Unfortunately, there is less time for families to grow, harvest, purchase, and prepare fresh foods. People continue to eat more high-calorie foods with low nutritional value. Currently, food companies are starting to fortify these foods with many of the essential nutrients, such as vitamins C, D, and E, calcium, iron, magnesium, and potassium. It's interesting because in preparing foods for mass consumption, the food companies have to ensure that the food won't spoil. So they take a natural food and extract much of its good nutritional value and add countless preservatives and additives to ensure good taste and long shelf life. The general public has been indifferent on this issue for many years, but currently there is a consumer trend toward more natural foods. Moreover, the customer is willing to pay a premium for these foods, so the food companies are responding by adding essential nutrients back into these processed foods.

Milk is a good example. Both children and adults around the world drink milk. There is currently a consumer trend toward purchasing and drinking organic milk. The average consumer is learning more about how milk is prepared. What they have learned is that often cows are given hormones and antibiotics during their life stages. The concern is that many of these medications or their by-products are passed into the milk found on the store shelves. Now that the consumer is aware of this issue with milk, they are choosing more natural forms of milk, which are more nutrient dense. In essence consumers are voting for more natural food choices, and they are voting with their spending money. This push toward giving the consumer better choices with milk is currently seen in the United States. The demand has been so significant that many large chain supermarkets offer it at a premium price. But even at a higher price, the consumer is willing to pay for a healthier choice in their milk. This organic milk generally has more of the good nutrients and less of the additives. If there is a demand for something, there will be a supply. So the good news here is that as the consumer demands more nutrient-dense foods, the market will respond with better choices.

CALORIE CONTROL

Calorie control is the biggest problem we face currently worldwide. So until we begin to control our calories, the problem will inevitably get worse before it gets better! There are many different health campaigns designed to raise awareness of the consumer. Unfortunately, we continue to watch the worldwide prevalence rates of obesity continue to climb. The companies who are progressive will stay ahead of the curve and be able to capitalize on this consumer trend.

Knowing the amount of calories in any food is always helpful information. Many fast-food companies are attempting to raise awareness by adding calorie counts on the menus next to the selections. This certainly is a positive step in the right direction. Hopefully calorie counts will help to raise consumer awareness of nutrition. The challenge lies in understanding exactly what is appropriate.

The general public has little understanding of what 1,000 calories for a cheeseburger means or 700 calories for a café latte. There is widespread ignorance in this area, from the doctors to their patients. People are eating and drinking excessive amounts of calories without knowing their own personal caloric requirements. This is why it's so important to start simple. Everyone needs a basic approach to understanding diet and nutrition. This approach has to start with an understanding of need.

KNOW YOUR FUEL NEEDS

What does the human body need? Most of you don't know how many daily calories you actually need to get through the typical day. However, you do know how much gas you need to get somewhere in your cars. When you shop for an automobile, you often look first at the information presented on the window of the car. One of the most important highlights of that information is the gas mileage, how much gas that car needs to travel a certain distance. Knowing the fuel needs will help to explain how much money you will spend on gasoline every month. It also helps to determine activity level. For example, if you drive a far distance to work, you will often purchase a car that has very good gas mileage. Not only is the price of filling up the fuel tank less expensive, it is also more practical to have a fuel-efficient car in this case. Economy cars such as the new hybrids are very attractive because they need very little gasoline to travel a long way. Other cars such as sport utility vehicles require a large amount of fuel because of their large engines. With a car purchase, every consumer knows the amount of gas a car requires to travel a certain distance.

We should have a fundamental understanding of our own fuel needs. We all know approximately how far our car will travel on a full tank of gas. But most of us have no idea how much fuel the average person needs to put in their body to get through the day. Just like a car, it depends on body size. People with economy car–like bodies require a small amount of fuel. So a woman of petite stature, whether old or young, may only need approximately

1,200 calories to get through the day. Conversely, people with SUV-like bodies require a large amount of fuel. An example would be a tall man with a muscular build, who would require more calories for function and maintenance of that body. Just like a car engine, the human body needs a specific amount of fuel for performance. We all should understand our own personal fuel needs.

Once you understand how much fuel you need, the next step is to choose the right type of fuel. At the fuel pump, there are numbers that define the purity or octane of the fuel. Every consumer knows that the higher the number, the better the fuel grade. So a gasoline score of 92 is higher in purity than an 87. This grading system is analogous to the type of calories in the diet. Much like that of gasoline, food has a relative nutrient composition.

As mentioned earlier, you need to choose foods with a high nutrient density, just as you choose a high-octane gasoline. For gasoline, high octane translates to higher automobile engine performance. With food, higher nutrient density translates to better human body performance. Nutrient-dense foods are packed with vitamins, minerals, trace elements, and antioxidants. The higher the nutrient density, the more of these good nutrients are available. For example, although they are small in size, blueberries are nutrient dense. Blueberries have unique antioxidant characteristics that have been shown to have protective effects for the eyes. Many eye doctors recommend blueberries in the daily diet to help protect against macular degeneration. Half a cup of blueberries has fewer than 100 calories and is packed with good nutrients. There are so many good food choices. So make sure to choose nutrient-dense foods that are relatively low in calories.

For a list of high-nutrient dense foods and conversely high-calorie, low-nutrient dense foods, see Appendix A, page 191.

SURROUNDED BY SUGAR

I always encourage my patients, when shopping, to avoid sugar and instead look for protein. Since we live in a carbohydrate-rich society, it's not always easy to find low-calorie, healthful foods, which are are generally expensive with a short shelf life. This is all too obvious when traveling. Whether it's the airport or a gas station, high-protein foods that are low in sugar are difficult to find. The next time you walk into a gas station, a food stop, or a snack bar in the airport, look around. You will see lots of chips, candies, crackers, doughnuts, muffins, and plenty of soda. Generally, the only protein is beef jerky, almonds, and milk. Now protein bars are coming into fashion, but they are not widespread. The problem that snacking on these sugary foods is the empty calories. You want to make your calories count, and sugar doesn't help much. Prepackaged foods that are high in sugar generally do not have a high nutrient density.

Protein is the nutrient of interest for most of the current diets. In the 1980s, the high-carbohydrate diet was king, but this diet has proven deleterious to most people. We do need carbohydrates—remember, it's like the fuel you add in the gas tank of your car—but unless you're training for a marathon, you do not need that much. Generally, about 40 to 50 percent of your daily calories can come from carbohydrates, which means on a 2,000-calorie-per-day diet, that is approximately 800 to 1,000 calories, which translates into the typical Western breakfast of a large latte and a muffin. Under these conditions, you're usually tapped out by 10 A.M. with all the carbs you need for the day. Now imagine adding some pizza, a hamburger, and a soda, a mid-afternoon coffee, a bag of chips . . . then maybe some bread with dinner. It's not hard to quickly accumulate 4,000 calories. Cutting carbohydrates out of the diet is the basis of most if not all of the popular diet programs today.

The idea of a low-fat diet has changed, and now a diet rich in healthy fats such as monounsaturated fats from nuts, avocados, and olive oil, and polyunsaturated fats from fish oil and flaxseed is popular. The percentage of dietary protein can vary widely, but most experts target around 30 percent.

FOCUS ON DIET

We will deal with exercise later in the book. But we can start with the basics of nutrition. I actually agree with most of the popular contemporary diets because most of them carry the same message and focus on the same two principles: controlling calories and reducing dietary sugar.

EAT 2,000, NOT 3,000

"Eat 2,000, not 3,000" simply means that if the average person needs approximately 2,000 calories or less, they are most likely eating 3,000 or more. The key is to focus on eating less than 2,000 calories per day, which is becoming more and more challenging.

ALMOST 2 BILLION PEOPLE OVERWEIGHT!

Every day the world is getting bigger. As stated earlier, the World Health Organization (WHO) reports 1.6 billion people worldwide being at least overweight. The concerning thing is that this number is most likely underreported. Because this estimate is conservative, there may be well over two billion people currently overweight, with the world's population approximately 6.7 billion. That means 30 percent or more of the entire world is most likely overweight.

Why is this? To keep it simple, we refer back to diet and exercise. In the past, we had better nutrition and performed more physical activity. This helped keep us in caloric balance. When the body has more calories than it requires, it stores them. Imagine taking your car to the gas station. You fill up the gas tank to the limit. If you continue to put gasoline in the fuel tank, it will spill out. The human body does not work that way. Instead of losing that extra fuel, the body actually stores it, even after the tank is full. This ability to store more calories was good for humans for thousands of years when food was scarce. In modern times with fast food, this works against us.

The diet changed dramatically after the Industrial Revolution. With factories and conveyor belts, we started packaging food so that it could sit on shelves for later consumption. We did not have to go to the market daily. We could shop once a week, or even less. Foods that can remain for extended periods of time on a shelf are generally higher in calories. The shift in diet toward higher-calorie foods brought with it a shift away from good nutrition. Most prepackaged foods are not high in nutrients. The industrial age caused a major shift in diet worldwide. This explains the diet, what about the exercise? Habits regarding physical activity have changed dramatically over the years. Worldwide, societies have increased the number of labor-saving devices. This means that globally humans physically are burning fewer calories. Technology has allowed machines to do much of the work that kept us in caloric balance. Traditionally, we worked on farms from early in the morning until late at night. Maintaining a good level of energy throughout the day meant that we had to start the day with a big breakfast. The traditional big breakfast has continued in many countries, but the physical activity is no longer necessary. As machines do much of our farming for us, we do not need to perform at the same level of activity as before. The problem is that the traditional big breakfast still remains in many countries, which sets up so many people for obesity. This is another challenge that youngsters are facing because parents are loading their children up in the morning with a large breakfast, typically full of sugar. Even worse, as time is becoming more and more limited, they may be taking their kids through the fast-food drive-throughs for the breakfast meals. These meals are typically loaded with sugars and fats, and very low in good vitamins, minerals, fiber, and antioxidants.

THE ROMAN EMPIRE DID NOT HAVE THE INTERNET

The age of information technology also caused a trend away from physical activity. Treadmills did not exist in ancient Rome, but Romans probably performed far more physical activity than present day societies. Imagine the amount of energy that went into the daily activities such as farming and construction. Today, these activities are performed by machines, but in years past, we did the vast majority of the work. Most people in past societies worked as physical laborers and ate sparingly. This meant that we burned far more calories than we do today. It was a necessity then, but it's not now. As technology continues to bring us advancements in almost all areas of life, we are performing less and less physical work. Which means that the average human is burning fewer and fewer calories every day.

It's quite amazing, but when you consider it, for hundreds of thousands of years, there were no overweight societies. Even in the lavish, decadent empires of thousands of years past, there were few obese people as a percentage of the total. There may have been an overweight few, who were wealthy enough to sit around and eat all day. The Roman Empire lacked both refrigerators and Internet access. Ancient Romans ate sparingly and physically labored. This meant that they were constantly burning more calories than they were consuming, which kept them in balance.

We have seen a worldwide shift to a "service economy." As previously mentioned, this is the how technology has affected our work habits. More people provide services via the Internet and telephone, rather than having to perform physical duties as part of their jobs. There is no doubt the introduction of labor-saving devices has helped us in many ways. However, they are creating an environment in which we physically move less. This means fewer calories being burned on a daily basis.

With these rapid changes in technology, we have seen dramatic changes in both diet and exercise, over a short period of time. To reverse this worldwide process, we must take simple steps toward improvement. So remember, it's the combination of inactivity and high-calorie food that has produced more overweight people, causing the worldwide pandemic of obesity.

THE GOOD NEWS

The good news is that this problem is preventable and reversible. Everyone can achieve good health through basic diet and exercise. It starts with educating yourself and taking simple steps in the right direction.

THE DIET ISN'T WORKING:
MAYBE I GAINED WEIGHT FROM WATER AND AIR!

Often patients tell me that their diet plan is not working and that they've gained weight. When I ask them how they gained weight, they often tell me that they've been drinking too much water or that they're bloated from gas, which together have added body weight. Water and gas can indeed cause weight gain, but generally not much in healthy people. People with diseases such as congestive heart failure or kidney failure can fluctuate tremendously with body weight. For the average healthy person, however, water and air have nothing to do with weight gain. Weight gain is generally caused by increased caloric consumption. Simply stated: weight is a function of the calories taken in and the calories burned. Although this looks simplistic, it's always good to review the following statement:

More calories = weight gain

Fewer calories = weight loss

To understand the calories consumed, one must understand what people are eating. To understand what people are eating, it's necessary to review the diet. People generally underreport what they've eaten and overreport their physical activity, so it's important to carefully document everything from meals to snacks to beverages. The first thing I start with is a dietary recall. In the office, I sit down with each patient and review the last three days of foods and beverages. From this, I calculate the average number of calories consumed. The average caloric consumption is generally well over 3,000 per day. So after careful review, I can target the areas of hidden calories. It's often the morning snacks like coffee and muffins or afternoon snacks like chips and sodas. With these dietary reviews, I help my patients understand where the calories are coming from. This makes them more educated consumers both in the markets and restaurants.

So many doctors become angry with their patients who are having difficulty losing or maintaining a healthy weight. The doctors believe that the patient is cheating, not sticking to the diet. And so often, the doctors accuse the patient of falling off track. This is the wrong approach. The blame game never works toward treating a problem. The issue is often ignorance of what to eat and what exercise to do. Again, the best method is to keep it simple for the individual so that he or she can achieve the goals put forth. First review the diet, then make simple diet recommendations.

THE FIRST LAW OF THERMODYNAMICS

There is a law of physics that all humans live by called *thermodynamics*. It's impossible to cheat this law, best explained by the phrase "energy is neither created nor destroyed, it's transferred."

How does this physics law apply to diet? When people are confused as to how they gained weight, I always explain that the energy must have come from somewhere. Fat does not spontaneously appear on the hips and stomach. Fat is energy storage and it contains calories. Calories cannot come from the air we breathe or the water we drink. Simply put, added weight comes from food.

Think about it this way. You cannot sit on the couch, eat nothing, and gain 10 pounds. The energy in those 10 pounds must originate from somewhere. It may sound simplistic, but it's a very important thing to understand.

I often use the law of thermodynamics in the clinical setting. Simply stated, weight gain occurs when more calories are consumed and fewer calories are burned. Remember, it's impossible to gain fat weight from water and air; it's always the hidden calories in food.

ARE YOU TRYING TO GET FAT?

You generally are not trying to eat more to gain weight. It's not premeditated weight gain, for sure. But the problem rests with consumer ignorance in food choices, the lack of education from us doctors, and the lack of explanation from the food companies.

WELL ADAPTED TO STARVATION

So the calories may be hidden or ignored, but always stored. When the body sees a calorie, the body holds onto that calorie for dear life.

Our ancestors were well adapted to starvation. This means that as a species, we do fine if we don't eat regularly, because that's how we operated for hundreds of thousands of years. We woke up, gathered fruits and vegetables, and hunted for wild game like meat or fish. We did not sit down to eat three meals a day at the dinner table. We often went days without a large meal, so our bodies adapted by having the ability to store and conserve calories. This adaptation of the human body was for survival when food was scarce.

RIGHT GENES, WRONG CENTURY

A very obese person is very well adapted to starvation. People who are morbidly obese have a very efficient method for storing calories in the body. The ability to store more fuel in the body is good. Thousands of years ago, men and women who required less food survived longer. Obese people tend to hold onto muscle better which is a genetic advantage. This means thousands of years ago, people who could hold onto fat and muscle better, lived longer. Think of obese people having the "right genes." Take those people and put them in a modern-day environment where food is plentiful and exercise is not necessary.

Think of modern times as the "wrong century" for people who efficiently store calories. The genetic advantage becomes a disadvantage because the environment works against the overweight individual. This is a recipe for obesity. Obese people in modern times often have medical conditions such as diabetes and hypertension. In ancient times, these same people who are obese today would have been very healthy. In fact, they probably would have been the leaders of ancient societies, muscular and resistant to starvation.

Being able to store more fuel in the body was a very good thing years ago. Unfortunately, modern day is a time of food abundance. To explain the phenomenon of obesity, think the "right genes" in the "wrong century."

THE CHALLENGE OF CONTROL

It's a beautiful genetic advantage for survival. In times past, when food was not so plentiful, it might have been days before the next major meal. Our bodies have adapted the ability to hold on to calories very efficiently for survival. Mother Nature has never provided a sustained abundance of calories to humans. Industrialization brought in technological advances in the food supply. Because of the advancements in food preparation, preservation, and packaging, most societies have available calories in one form or another.

Even in poorer countries, where many suffered from starvation, obesity-related chronic diseases are replacing the infectious diseases from years ago. The challenge that lies ahead for us as a global society will be to control the calories in our food supply so that countries with very large populations don't suffer the consequences of overweight citizens. The way it looks now, we are not stopping. The expansion of fast food restaurants worldwide is moving at an alarming rate. And most of the fast-food restaurants are not concerned with controlling calories. In fact, many of these fast-food restaurants are selling the idea of more food for less money. Of course more food means more calories in the body. And of course, our bodies will continue to hold onto extra calories, which we encounter in our environment. The solution in this situation is to control the incoming calories. In doing this, we maintain our health and reap the genetic benefits that Mother Nature bestowed upon us.

SO, WHAT DO I EAT?

The vast majority of books on diet and exercise have extensive lists of recommended menus and suggested ways to prepare food. Working with some of the best clinical dieticians, I have listed some basic diet recommendations that will help control the calories and cut the sugar. There are many ways to maintain a diet rich in healthy nutrients and low in calories.

To keep it simple, I have listed some suggested meal plans, which my patients found to be easy and effective. They are basic and they are based on different caloric plans: 1,200 calories, 1,500 calories, and 1,800 calories (see Appendix B, p. 199).

You will notice a meal replacement listed within the recommended foods. Within the modern-day context of this worldwide problem of obesity, one of the most important developments has been the meal replacement.

CONSIDER MEAL REPLACEMENTS

What Is a Meal Replacement?

Imagine taking your typical breakfast meal with eggs, bacon, fruit, toast, juice, and milk and mixing all these contents into a blender. Now take out all the bad fat and most of the sugar, just leaving the protein, vitamins, minerals, fiber, good fat, and healthy antioxidants. Well, that's basically what a meal replacement is. It's "engineered food" that is generally packed with nutrients but lower in calories. To be called a true meal replacement, it must fit the profile of one. Which means it must have certain amounts of key nutrients per serving.

Meal replacements come in many forms, such as prepackaged shakes, bars, soups, even cookies! All of these satisfy the requirements of a meal. For most people, a meal replacement helps to support a healthy weight. But even for athletes and thin individuals, a meal replacement will ensure healthy nutrients in the diet.

Meal replacements are one of the simplest methods for guaranteeing a healthy meal, while taking the guesswork out of eating.

Gaining Control

The great thing about a meal replacement is that it does not lie when it comes to calories. If the label states: mix with water and you will get 200 calories, then you will receive 200 calories when you consume it. Meal replacements are useful for doctors and dieticians who work in a clinical setting where calories must be measured accurately. Moreover, they are convenient in designing a diet plan with times throughout the day. Individuals have different eating patterns. So meal replacements help individualize the diet program.

Meal replacements are incredibly helpful for those of you who have tried and failed various diet programs for years and have become comfortable with failure. Often patients come to me in the clinical setting and report that they've tried everything, and they are on their last attempt. For these individuals, the meal replacement is great. It takes all the mystery out of counting calories in the diet and keeps the program simple.

One of the most powerful things meal replacements can enable you to accomplish is to allow you to gain control of your own dietary habits. Moreover, you will do not feel as though you are starving yourself or limiting your calories. When you feel hungry, simply choose another meal replacement or nutrient dense snack and you will know exactly how many calories you've consumed. This helps tremendously in two ways for in monitoring your diet. First, it allows you to count your calories without having to guess a general amount. Second, it gives you more power in the planning process of your own nutrition program.

So often in speaking with my patients, they tell me that they were doing well, and then they ate something with high calories and felt as though they "lost it." When they go off the diet once, many completely give up on their entire program because they're not sure of what they are doing. They are conscious of the fact that they deviated from their personal program, but they don't know to what degree. By eating foods like meal replacements and other nutrient-dense snacks, you can know exactly the number of calories you are consuming. This helps you continually plan your program. A good example of a situation where you could control calories would be a wedding. If you knew ahead of time that you were going to a wedding and that you'd be eating a good amount of food, you could prepare during the week by limiting your calories well within healthy limits, and still have some room to deviate on the day of the wedding.

Wouldn't it be great if food always came with nutritional information attached, even at restaurants and social events? It would certainly take much of the guesswork out of the dieting. It's not as though most people are trying to find foods that are higher in calories. Consumers often have the best of intentions when making food choices in social settings. But their nutritional fate is in someone else's hands. A major challenge is that the individual starts with the best of intentions but cannot control the amount of calories in the meals. Once they've ordered their food at a restaurant, the chef will determine everything else.

THE CHEF IS NOT YOUR DOCTOR

Do people lie about what they've eaten? Not really. The problem is not dishonesty, its ignorance.

In the clinical setting, my patients often ask for dietary guidance. Many prefer not to eat any type of engineered food, particularly meal replacements, as they feel they are too synthetic. Physicians should always respect their patients' respective wishes and strive to personalize their nutrition for them. The problem is not with the doctor or the patient, it's often beyond control. The problem lies in the process of food preparation.

Let's take a typical clinical scenario. An individual asks for dietary guidance, and I recommend eating specific fresh foods. As an example, I recommend eating grilled chicken breast for lunch, but there is no telling what may be in the actual meal. A typical large piece of grilled white chicken over an assortment of fresh vegetables should not be more than 300 calories. But what most people get in a typical restaurant is a grilled chicken salad with well over 800 calories, most of them hidden in the sauces and dressing.

If you go out to eat and order the grilled chicken salad, often what you get is a high-fat, high-sugar, calorie-packed meal. Remember, your chef is not your doctor. Even though you've requested a grilled chicken breast, the chef is not concerned about your cholesterol level or your weight. Generally the chef is concerned with your taste buds and your wallet. That chef wants you to enjoy your meal so that you will tell your friends about that restaurant. Remember, the chef is not your doctor.

So preparing a low-fat, low-sugar, grilled chicken breast over salad is not what you would expect. The special sauces are added to liven up the taste of the chicken, which means more calories into your body, often unbeknownst to you. Remember some of the simple diet rules from previous chapters. Focus on 2,000 calories per day. For example, you only need 2,000 calories per day, and for breakfast you've already had a very large latte with a blueberry muffin (total of 1,200 calories, mostly sugar). Now for lunch, you order the grilled chicken breast salad (with the special honey mustard dressing, croutons, and cheese at 800 calories). Now it's about 1:00 in the afternoon. You still have hours to go at work, which means the mid-afternoon snack, probably another cup of coffee, an energy drink, or a soda. After all of this, you head home to prepare a full meal or order fast food. You can see how blowing by 3,000 calories a day is not hard to do. After several weeks of this dietary pattern, you either gain weight or do not lose weight as desired. You may return to speak with your clinical nutrition specialist and complain that the diet you've been following does not work. Often you are angry because you've radically changed your dietary habits to fit the specialist's program. You may feel both the diet and the specialist have failed you, and this often creates a feeling of hopelessness. This is why so many people have difficulties with their diet plans: they simply do not know what they are consuming. The blame rests in many places, including the consumer and the nutrition specialist, but a large portion rests in the area of food preparation and production.

Why Would a Doctor Recommend Meal Replacements?

As a clinical nutrition doctor, I have been recommending meal replacements to my patients for many years. I often do press interviews on dieting and nutrition, and the inevitable question from reporters is this: "Why not recommend natural whole foods? Meal replacements are not natural; they are synthetic . . . so why give them to your patients?" They are absolutely correct. And I always state the obvious: the food Mother Nature has created is better than anything made at a food company. The problem is that very few people are eating what Mother Nature prepared for us.

SOCIETY IS NOT HELPING

Eating healthy foods is a challenge to the average consumer, and society is generally working against the consumer. I do not believe that it is some preconceived conspiracy by the food companies to fatten us up. It's just the path of least resistance. If a typical one- or two-parent family works many hours to just make ends meet, it's often difficult to prepare fresh food when they've finished work.

I am recommending cutting sugar calories and focusing on consuming around 2,000 calories, which is a worldwide standard seen on food labels. There is also a danger in having too few calories, so I often encourage my patients to balance nutrients in the diet and just cut calories from sugar. History has shown that there have been problems with low-calorie diets. With too few calories, the body cannot receive sufficient nutrients for proper functioning of daily activities. This is similar to having a very expensive luxury car, but putting in very little fuel, very little oil, or very little transmission fluid. Without the proper component, any machine can break down. Because of this, medical doctors have defined very low calories by certain numbers.

THE VERY LOW-CALORIE DIET (VLCD)

I am advocating cutting calories in the diet and looking for foods packed with nutrients. We must eat some food of course. We can't starve ourselves and expect to perform. There is a serious problem in restricting calories too much. In the clinical setting, if I put a patient on a diet lower than 800 calories per day, then I will medically monitor them. The medical definition of a very low-calorie diet is one under 800 calories daily. It is possible to keep these patients on a very low-calorie diet for quite an extended period of time, but the nutrients must be packed into the diet and the protein must be complete. (A complete protein is one that has all the essential amino acids in it.)

REMEMBER: CUT CALORIES

Remember, calories are the biggest culprit in this worldwide pandemic of obesity that is growing out of control. Remember the 2,000-calorie count you will see on food labels worldwide. People are consuming far more than that, usually about 3,000 or more. This is of course supported by the ever-increasing prevalence rates of overweight and obesity in every westernized country in the world. The basic step of calorie control is the success behind every major diet currently on the market. That is why so many people start on a diet and lose a significant amount of weight, only to return to their old ways of eating those hidden calories. We need to educate the consumer on these issues so that they can make wiser food choices as it pertains to their overall health.

THE YO-YO DIET

You will hear it every time: "That diet worked for only eight weeks, then I gained all my weight back, and even more!" This is the phenomenon of the yo-yo diet. Historically, the major problem with dieting has been the limiting of calories without adequate protein intake. When you simply cut calories, the important nutrients are often left out of the diet. Remember, your muscles are made of protein. When we do not eat protein, we lose vital muscle mass. Remember fat is an efficient form of energy storage. Our bodies are simply conditioned for survival, to store as many calories as possible. When we yo-yo, we cut our daily calories in the diet, which often lacks sufficient protein to support the muscle. So we lose weight quickly, yes! We may lose 20 pounds in a month . . . but that's mostly water and muscle, not fat.

FAT HOLDS ON TIGHT

If anything, fat is tenacious, holding on for dear life. As soon as you go back to your typical eating pattern—high calories, high sugar, high fat—you gain all the muscle back and often a little more fat. This is the vicious cycle of the yo-yo diet. Most of the current diets are relatively sufficient in protein, all targeting around 30 percent of total calories in the diet, some a little more, some a little less. It's the problem of sticking to the plan and figuring out what works for you.

So we know the problem, what's the solution? Yes, you guessed it . . . more protein in the diet. I have been an advocate of higher protein diets for years, but the nutritional philosophy that I studied promotes a healthy balance of animal and plant protein sources. The mix can be 50/50 animal to plant protein. The key here is once again to cut calories, and choose foods that are high in protein.

FOCUS ON PROTEIN

Humans cannot survive without protein. I always tell my patients, without protein, we will certainly die. What's more, we can not physically make protein from other nutrients in the diet.

EAT PROTEIN OR DIE

We must eat complete proteins in the diet, which means that we must eat foods that have all the essential amino acids. Amino acids are the building blocks of tissues in our bodies. We make

---

THE ESSENTIAL AMINO ACIDS

- Phenylalanine
- Histidine
- Arginine
- Methionine
- Leucine
- Tryptophan
- Valine
- Threonine
- Isoleucine
- Lysine

---

some amino acids in the body, but there are others that we do not make. Those amino acids that we cannot produce as humans, we must eat. They are called *essential amino acids* because they are *essential* to our survival.

FOCUS ON PROTEIN FIRST—
TAKE CARE OF YOUR ENGINE

Protein has many functions, one of the most important of which is maintaining lean muscle mass. Remember, your body is like an engine, and protein is the building block of structure for the engine. Without protein, your body's engine breaks down structurally.

Using the analogy of a car, think of protein as the heavy architecture that supports the body of the car, the brakes, the transmission, the engine, the struts, and so on. People who own cars often take the cars into the shop for basic servicing. We should think the same way about our bodies.

WE ONLY GET ONE BODY

In the car shop, we can replace parts in our cars if they are damaged. Unfortunately, we only have one body and no spare parts to replace if damaged. These are the building blocks of the body's individual organ systems. People often ask me about protein amounts in the diet, and if they are consuming too much. One thing is for sure, if we do not eat protein, we do not live. Protein is one of the three macronutrients. There are truly three macronutrients: proteins, carbohydrates, and fats. All three are essential to good health. Alcohol is sometimes thought of as a fourth nutrient, but it offers no nutritive value, and one cannot survive alone on alcohol. Each of the three major macronutrients stores calories.

THE THREE MAJOR MACRONUTRIENTS: PROTEIN, CARBOHYDRATES, AND FATS

If we look at one gram of each of these nutrients, we can see how much energy they store. This is where nature gets really interesting. One gram of protein holds approximately 4 calories of energy. That's what Mother Nature decided it would be, so if you eat an energy bar that says 10 grams of protein on it, that means protein is providing 40 calories of energy. Carbohydrates hold the same amount of calories per gram at 4.

But fat is incredibly good at storing energy, which is why it's so tough to get rid of fat. Our bodies generally want to hold onto fat because it's such an efficient form of energy storage. One gram of fat holds 9 calories, that's two and a half times a comparable amount of protein and carbohydrates hold.

In ancient times, fat storage was paramount to get through the long winters when food was scarce. You must remind yourself that drive-ins were not around in the Paleolithic Age, so the image of Fred Flintstone picking up a side of ribs in the drive-through was not quite accurate.

The three macronutrients all have different functions but they must work together in the body for optimal health.

NO PLACE TO STORE PROTEIN

Although sugar and fat get stored quite efficiently, protein does not have a reservoir or a depot where it can hang out. When we eat sugar, it gets digested and stored as glycogen, which is the starch form. We store this sugar in our muscles and our liver. When we eat fat, we store it in the extensive adipose tissue depots throughout the body. Even the thinnest people have tons of fat storage that we cannot see. But protein is different.

When we eat protein, we don't store it. Protein gets processed by the body and broken down into component amino acids. These amino acids have many different functions in the body. As mentioned earlier, one major function is to support the lean muscle mass in the legs, arms, back, abdominals, and so on. Even the tiny muscles in the face need protein for support. The amino acids get processed by the body, and if necessary, get incorporated into the muscle tissue for growth and repair. If the body's muscles don't need protein, it doesn't get stored. This process is quite different than that of sugar and fat. If the body sees sugar and fat, it gets stored. It's like a big well that gets deeper and deeper the more sugars and fats that we eat.

MUSCLE BREAKDOWN

When an athlete finishes a workout, his or her muscles have been challenged and need more protein building blocks, those amino acids, to help rebuild the tissue. It's as if the car's frame has been a bit damaged, and it constantly needs a little repair. This is how protein works.

LOOKING FOR PROTEIN

Because we do not store protein the way we store sugars and fats, we must find constant sources of protein, whether they be from vegetable or animal. Sources of vegetable protein include legumes, soy, rice, peas, and beans. Animal sources include chicken, turkey, beef, pork, and fish.

CLINICAL EVIDENCE FOR THE POWER OF PROTEIN

In a clinical research study, we compared high-protein diets to relatively lower protein diets. Those who ate more protein lost more fat weight and maintained more muscle.

This is a testament to the power of protein. Protein is more satisfying than sugars or fats, which is a good thing when one is on a weight-management program.

And remember, protein does not store a lot of calories so it satisfies the hunger and maintains the body's muscle mass and tissues, without creating a large amount of calories in the diet.

The power of protein—don't forget it.

HOW MUCH PROTEIN SHOULD I EAT?

How much protein should we eat daily? This is controversial, and different countries have different recommendations, but the general recommendations for survival are around 50 grams for women and 60 grams for men. Now considering this is the amount one would need to survive, that does seem like much. Not long ago, many of the dieticians in the hospital I worked with as a medical student would recommend approximately 0.8 gram of protein per kilogram body weight, which has now changed to approximately 1 gram of protein per kilogram of body weight. This can be confusing to calculate. Often, a quick easy reference may help the average person more than the calculations. In the clinical setting, I recommend approximately 75 grams for women and 100 grams for men. And here's the great addition, about half of that protein can be from vegetable sources and half from animal sources. This provides a good balance in the diet rather than having all of the protein from steak, for example. So remember to get sufficient protein in the diet to support all of your body's structures.

PROTEIN IS THE BEST MACRONUTRIENT

Protein is well accepted as an important macronutrient because it satisfies hunger and supports muscle. It is unique in that there is an inherent metabolic tax on it. This means the body has to work harder to process protein in the diet than it does for sugars and fats. To simplify, imagine eating 100 calories of sugar. Anytime we eat anything, the human body must perform work to digest and assimilate. This means it takes work for the body to eat. This process is called the thermogenic effect of food. Simply put, the body has to work, even when we're eating. And every nutrient requires a certain amount of energy to digest. It turns out that the body burns more calories working on protein than it does for sugars and fats. From the time you place those 100 calories in your mouth, to the point at which those sugars are incorporated into your cells for fuel energy or storage, you may burn only 2 to 5 calories. Which means of the 100 sugar calories you've eaten, you've absorbed about 95 of them. This is even worse for fats. With fat, we use 1 to 2 calories. Again fat is an efficient storage form of energy. It doesn't take a lot of energy to store fat, but it does to burn it.

PROTEIN LIVES IN THE HIGHEST TAX BRACKET

Protein is unique because of its chemical structure. No wonder these high-protein diets work, they force the body to burn more calories while you're eating. Think of this as the metabolic tax on food. Yes, that's correct, even food has a tax bracket! And protein lives in the highest bracket, which is great for us because we are getting the three-for-one special with protein: increased satisfaction, muscle support, and high metabolic tax. Many critics say that protein can be unhealthy, which makes little sense to me because protein has been around for millions of years, so why would nature provide us with something unhealthy? The myth of protein damaging the kidneys has been purported, but not well substantiated in scientific literature. Of course, too much of anything is bad, even protein. Most diets recommend eating protein as approximately 30 percent of the total daily calories. I recommend 30 percent in the diet, which is a relatively conservative number. Moreover, I recommend eating protein from both vegetable and animal sources, so the body has variety. Science has proven protein to be healthy time and time again, reinforcing the notion that plant with animal protein is good for a healthy diet. Without the essential amino acids in the diet, the human body breaks down.

PROTEIN MALNUTRITION AND BROKEN HEARTS

A significant example of protein malnutrition in developed countries is anorexia nervosa. This medical condition has been studied for many years ago and has caused significant problems for many young people, predominantly women.

With anorexia, the ultimate challenge is that too little protein can cause death. With fewer calories in the diet, especially protein calories, the body takes more and more protein from the muscle tissue.

After losing a significant amount of protein from muscle, the body takes protein from other organs in the body. Usually the last resort is to take protein from the most vital muscle in the body—the heart.

Often when they try to control their weight by taking in very few calories per day, it wreaks havoc on the body's systems. Because these few calories do not add up to complete nutrients, these individuals suffer more from malnutrition.

When the heart muscle gets attacked for protein, the heart faces serious challenges. With extreme protein malnutrition, death from heart attacks can ensue. There is no good reason for a young person to die an untimely death from major malnutrition and protein deprivation, whether in a developed or underdeveloped country.

So back to calories. Remember, we need around 2,000 but we're eating more than 3,000. This is the first major challenge. Controlling calories is the first key more than anything. Again, it's not tough to figure out when we start to see the number of overweight and obese individuals worldwide. As we try to get a handle on this out-of-control prevalence rates, just remember, it's the calories first and foremost! Most people do not have the problem of eating too few calories, so that's not a major issue, but eating a diet packed with protein, vitamins, minerals, fiber, and antioxidants can be challenging.

EAT 7 SERVINGS OF FRUITS AND VEGETABLES DAILY

D r. David Heber at UCLA wrote a book called *What Color Is Your Diet?* in which he describes the association of specific colored foods and the powerful healthy nutrients in them. For example, tomatoes fall into the red category, and they are rich in a compound called *lycopene*, known to be healthful. From blueberries to broccoli, Mom was correct in making us finish our fruits and veggies at the dining table. These foods have an abundance of powerful health-promoting nutrients called *phytonutrients* (*phyto* is the greek root word for "plant"). These plant nutrients build up in the fruits and vegetables often as antioxidant protection. We eat the plants and absorb the powerful, health-promoting nutrients.

Eating fruits and vegetables is not as common as it used to be. As societies worldwide join into the global economy, the modern lifestyle is changing the traditional diet. Many people no longer have time to pick their own fruit from their backyards or farms. Often, people do not have the time to shop at the market for fresh fruits and vegetables. With longer workdays and higher expectations for increased productivity, the traditional diet continues to change.

TWO MOST COMMONLY EATEN FRUITS AND VEGETABLES—FRENCH FRIES AND KETCHUP

Most doctors recommend at least five to seven servings of fruits and vegetables in the diet. But in most westernized societies, you will find the two most commonly eaten fruits and vegetables are the potatoes for French fries and tomatoes for the ketchup that the French fries are dipped in, a fact well documented in countries like the United States. This issue is extensively discussed in Eric Schlosser's book *Fast Food Nation*. This means that often fruit and vegetable servings three through seven are virtually nonexistent unless it's the lettuce on the hamburger that you're counting.

PROTECT YOUR CELLS

What's so great about fruits and vegetables? Unless you've been living in a cave, you've probably heard the term antioxidants by now. Throughout the day, the body is attacked by oxidative processes, best illustrated by cutting a piece of fruit in half and watching the inside of the fruit turn brown. Oxygen, sunlight, and various other factors cause oxidation. Specific nutrients in fruits and vegetables slow this process of oxidation down. For example, if you cut a piece of fruit in half, then squeeze lemon juice over the fruit, it will slow the process of it turning brown. The lemon has these natural antioxidants in it that we can absorb and make use of.

With powerful media campaigns, now more than ever, the public knows about antioxidants. When I was kid, there were commercials for different juices, but they never spoke of antioxidants. The words were not known to the public. Currently, it's the hottest ingredient to look for in foods and beverages. Even the major soda companies are adding antioxidants to their drinks.

Antioxidants are found in both plants and animals, but many of the plant antioxidants have been discovered to have major protective functions on the body's cells, a relatively recent discovery. Plants come in all shapes, sizes, and colors—from bright greens to strong yellows and reds. These plant pigments have various functions including protection from the oxidants in the environment. The sun is a major oxidant that beats down on plants daily with its UV rays and heat. The plants build up their defenses with these powerful antioxidants, which often manifest in these bright colors. The wonderful thing is that when we eat plants, we can absorb these wonderful antioxidants nature created for us, and they in turn can protect our cells from oxidant stress and damage. This is why scientists find such strong associations between healthy people and the consumption of fruits and vegetables. Of course the fiber, vitamins, and minerals contribute tremendously, but the antioxidants found throughout the plant kingdom are truly cellular protection.

How do we get protection for our cells in the diet? Oh, that's simple; just eat five to seven servings of fruits and vegetables daily. Some recommend even more which is fine, but a minimum of five to seven is best. Remember the French fries and ketchup as the most consumed fruits and vegetables? Those are clearly numbers 1 and 2, but after that, we don't see a tremendous amount of fruits and vegetable consumption in countries eating a Western diet, a problem seen in both adults and children. These two limited sources don't offer people a wide variety of antioxidants in the diet. As mentioned earlier, tomatoes do have a powerful antioxidant nutrient called lycopene, which has protective effects on the prostate gland in men and breast tissue in women. I never heard of lycopene when I was a kid, but now if you glance on the back of most tomato ketchup containers, you will notice the food companies touting its benefits. The only problem is the amount of unnecessary sugar in those bottles of ketchup.

So if we are eating an average of two servings of fruits and vegetables, where are the other five? Basically, they're not in the diet. You can't count the little pieces of lettuce and pickles on your typical hamburger.

Human cells are meant to eat all the wonderful antioxidant rich foods nature created. When you think back to the ancient diet, remember that we did not have fast food back then. We couldn't bake bread, fry meat, or cook noodles. Remember, we hunted and foraged for food. Since there was no butcher shop to visit for top sirloin, we mostly collected the fruits and vegetables available to us. If we did get fresh meat, fish, or foul, we couldn't refrigerate it, so we consumed it and moved on. With such an antioxidant-rich ancient diet, we know that we are currently way off the mark from where we used to be.

So how can we get back to where we were? Well, first very simply, we can eat those five to seven servings that we spoke of. Many of my clinic patients tell me that it's just too hard to consume with their hectic daily schedules. So what other options do we have?

Many supplement companies isolate the powerful antioxidants found in fruits and vegetables and usually package them in a tablet form for easy daily consumption, for example, the lutein in blueberries or the lycopene in tomatoes. Because these antioxidants, abundant in fruits and vegetables, have been discovered to have tremendous health benefits, I am a true believer in supplementing the diet with them. I think of them as a nutritional safety net in the daily diet. Although I always recommend eating what nature has provided for us—the best sources of fiber, antioxidants, vitamins, and minerals through natural fruits and vegetables—if you are eating the typical modern diet and are lacking essential nutrients, I recommend the next best thing: dietary supplements.

SUPPLEMENTS

Supplements are regarded as prepacked nutrients that help to support a healthy diet. Examples include vitamins, minerals, amino acids, antioxidants, fiber, protein powder, and ergogenic aids. As I said, I look at these forms of nutrition as a large nutritional safety net for consumers. There has undoubtedly been much controversy over the efficacy of supplements. Research on omega 3 fish oils shows them to be helpful in maintaining a healthy omega 3/6 ratio. They are supported by research. Just recently, vitamin D has been shown to be essential in a healthy diet as well (we make vitamin D from a certain amount of sun exposure). Many other supplements have been controversial, such as garlic. Just recently, a major research study questioned the healthy aspects of garlic on the heart. People will most likely continue to eat garlic and garlic supplements, although many research articles question their efficacy. In the following sections are lists of vitamins, minerals, and popular phytonutrients available in the marketplace.

VITAMINS

Vitamin A

Vitamin A is important for a variety of physiological functions including protecting the immune system. Vitamin A is one of the fat-soluble vitamins and serves as a powerful antioxidant. It helps to support healthy eye function by preventing macular degeneration and helps to fight infections in the body. Fat-soluble vitamins can build up in the fatty tissues of the body, while water-soluble vitamins are easily excreted. For this reason, vitamin A can be toxic in very high levels in the diet, especially in very young children. Good sources of vitamin A include spinach, pumpkin, yams, cantaloupe, and carrots.

Beta-Carotene

Beta-carotene is a precursor to vitamin A and serves as an antioxidant. Good sources of beta-carotene include spinach, green leafy vegetables, and apricots.

Vitamin B₁ (Thiamin)

Vitamin B$_1$ is also known as thiamin. A deficiency of this vitamin causes a condition known as beriberi, which is characterized by depression; memory impairment; difficulty with motor function such as walking; swelling in the peripheral tissues; and fatigue.

Good sources of Vitamin B$_1$ include oranges, beans, red meat, and pork.

Vitamin B₂ (Riboflavin)

Vitamin B$_2$, also known as riboflavin, helps with reproduction and growth of tissues, including hair, skin, and nails. It's a powerful antioxidant that has many functions throughout the body. Just as it helps with the growth of hair, skin, and nails, a deficiency will impair the growth of these tissues. Visual problems can also result from a deficiency of this vitamin.

Good sources of Vitamin B$_2$ include spinach, asparagus, broccoli, and yogurt.

Vitamin B₃ (Niacin)

Vitamin B_3, also known as niacin, helps to control and reduce triglyceride and cholesterol levels, support blood circulation, and maintain healthy blood pressure. It's an important vitamin, but excessive amounts may cause skin itching and flushing, diarrhea, nausea, headaches, and nervousness.

Good sources of Vitamin B_3 include veal, chicken, and tuna.

Vitamin B₅ (Pantothenic Acid)

Vitamin B_5, also known as panthothenic acid, helps to support healthy digestive functioning, healthy skin, and the production of hormones in the body. Good sources of Vitamin B_5 include eggs, mushrooms, pork, nuts, liver, and fish.

Vitamin B₆ (Pyridoxine)

Vitamin B_6, also known as pyridoxine, helps to support nerve tissues, neurotransmitters, and the metabolism of fatty acids in the body. Good sources of Vitamin B_6 include eggs, peanuts, avocados, red meat, chicken, and soybeans.

Vitamin B₁₂

Vitamin B_{12} is important in the production of red blood cells and nerve fibers in the body. Vitamin B_{12} deficiency may cause anemia and nervous tissue damage. Good sources include oysters, clams, crab, tuna, and salmon.

Biotin

Biotin, a complex of B vitamins, helps to support healthy skin and hair. Good sources of biotin include eggs and milk.

Folic Acid

Folic acid is another B vitamin that is probably best known for its role in preventing birth defects such as neural tube defects, such as Spina bifida. Folic acid helps to support the production of white blood cells, red blood cells, and nerve cells. It's also believed to reduce the risk of cancer and psychiatric disorders such as depression.

Good sources of folic acid include spinach, broccoli, asparagus, beans, okra, and brussels sprouts.

Vitamin C

Vitamin C serves as a powerful antioxidant in the body. It helps to support tissue healing and collagen growth. A deficiency of vitamin C in the diet can cause bleeding gums, muscle and joint pain, hemorrhages, and a condition known as scurvy.

Good sources of vitamin C include fruits and vegetables such as oranges, broccoli, cauliflower, tomatoes, red peppers, melons, and berries.

Vitamin D

Vitamin D is a fat-soluble vitamin that helps to support healthy bone growth and metabolism. It also helps support the body's fight against certain cancers such as breast cancer and prostate cancer. Vitamin D not only supports healthy bones, but healthy teeth as well. Vitamin D deficiency can cause a condition called rickets in which bone is malformed.

Good sources of Vitamin D include eggs, milk, tuna, salmon, halibut, and sardines. Sun exposure, even as little as 10 to 15 minutes, is another source of Vitamin D.

Vitamin E

Vitamin E, another fat-soluble vitamin that serves as an antioxidant, helps to support cellular functions, including blood clotting. It also helps to support nervous system tissues and eye health. Vitamin E is also believed to support cardiovascular health, respiratory function, and immune system activity. Good sources include spinach, seeds, and nuts.

Vitamin K

Vitamin K is a fat-soluble vitamin that is primarily involved in blood-clotting mechanisms.

Good sources include eggs, broccoli, green leafy vegetables, and soybeans.

MINERALS

Calcium

Calcium, an important mineral, is probably best known for its role in bone health. Calcium works with phosphorous, vitamin

D, and magnesium to help support bone health. Calcium also helps to support heart and nerve tissue function, blood-clotting mechanisms, and muscle contractions.

Good sources include broccoli, green leafy vegetables, salmon, sardines, and yogurt.

Chromium

Chromium is a mineral that helps to support healthy blood sugar levels in the body. It has been shown to help with weight loss because of its relation to blood glucose levels. Good sources of chromium include broccoli, brown rice, and pork.

Copper

Copper helps to support the growth of healthy bone, skin, and connective tissue. A deficiency of copper in the diet can lead to poor bone health. Good sources of copper include broccoli, avocados, mushrooms, almonds, green leafy vegetables, salmon, soybeans, and oysters.

Iodine

Iodine helps to support metabolism of the thyroid gland. Iodine is an important component of thryoid hormone, which helps to regulate body temperature and metabolism. A deficiency of iodine causes symptoms of hypothyroidism, including dry skin, constipation, weight gain, fatigue, and hair loss.

Good sources of iodine include spinach, shrimp, lobster, squash, and soybeans.

Magnesium

Magnesium is important in the body's metabolism. It's especially important in relation to calcium in the body for a variety of processes. Magnesium is involved in muscle activities, blood pressure regulation, and energy production.

Good sources include spinach, green leafy vegetables, blueberries, broccoli, avocados, and brown rice.

Manganese

Manganese is important for bone metabolism, central nervous system function, and collagen formation. Manganese deficiency can cause problems with vision and/or hearing as well as rapid heart rate and convulsions. Good sources of manganese include nuts, pineapple, avocados, eggs, blueberries, and shellfish.

Potassium

Potassium is an electrolye that works with sodium to regulate fluid balance in the body. Potassium deficiency can cause problems with blood pressure, heart rhythm function, nervous tissue function, and muscle contractions.

Good sources include spinach, avocados, bananas, raisins, apricots, brown rice, melon, and potatoes.

Selenium

Selenium is a powerful antioxidant and has been shown to support the elimination of free radicals. Selenium deficiency has been associated with certain cancers such as prostate, breast, and colon.

Good sources of selenium include broccoli, onions, tuna, brown rice, crab, and Brazil nuts.

Zinc

Zinc is a key component in the body's own natural antioxidants. Zinc helps to support protein metabolism and tissue healing. Deficiency of zinc has been shown to cause decreased immunity, which makes people more susceptible to colds.

Good sources of zinc include soybeans, nuts, whole grains, eggs, beef, and fish.

NATURAL NUTRIENTS

In addition to vitamins and minerals, there are other natural vital nutrients. Following is a group that I believe are important for health.

Alpha Lipoic Acid

Alpha lipoic acid is a powerful antioxidant in the body. Many nutrients are fat soluble, which means they comfortably exist in a fatty environment, while others are water soluble, meaning they are comfortable in aqueous environments. The interesting thing about alpha lipoid acid is that it can exist in both mediums. The body naturally makes this incredible antioxidant, but supporting a healthy diet with supplementation will help the body's metabolism.

Coenzyme Q10

Coenzyme Q10 is another antioxidant that is important for metabolism. It helps to support cardiovascular health, oral gum health, blood pressure, and immune system functioning. Taking certain medications like statins may cause levels of coenzyme Q10 to become depleted in the body.

Garlic

A powerful part of a healthy diet is garlic. An important compound in garlic is called *allicin*. It has been shown to support cardiovascular health, blood pressure, and immune system functioning. Many companies make garlic supplements, which are approximately equal to one clove of garlic.

Ginkgo Biloba

The herb ginko biloba has been associated with brain health, including memory. It is believed to support circulation to these important tissues in the brain. Ginkgo has powerful anticlotting activity in the blood and helps to support blood pressure.

Ginseng

Ginseng, an important herb associated with vitality and energy, helps to support blood pressure, stress, and depression. A recent clinical trial showed that combining ginseng with ginkgo can improve short-term memory and alertness.

Glucosamine

Glucosamine is associated with lubrication of joints in the body because of its role in mucous secretions. It supports the production and maintenance of connective tissues in the body.

Glutamine

Glutamine, a naturally occurring amino acid, is important in metabolism. Glutamine is especially important in protein metabolism and central nervous system functioning. A good source of glutamine is spinach.

Glutathione

Glutathione, a powerful antioxidant, helps to support healthy liver functioning, especially the detoxification process.

Grape Seed

The good stuff in wine is from the grapes. Remember that grapes have to sit long hours in the sun before they are harvested for consumption. During this time, they build up their own defenses from oxidative damage from the sun. This protection is the antioxidant in the grape. When humans consume grapes, they are able to absorb all the good stuff into their own cells. This again is cellular protection with all the good stuff that nature provided for us millions of years ago.

Green Tea

When we look at populations that consume a significant amount of green tea, there seems to be an association with good health: the more green tea, the more healthy the population. Studies have shown there are lower rates of cancer in populations that drink green tea regularly.

So what's so great about green tea? Well, we've discovered that there is a specific component called *EGCG*. The green tea molecules have cell-protective effects, which may help in the prevention of stomach and colon cancer.

They also have metabolic boosting effects, which have been shown to be stimulatory.

Drinking more tea throughout the day has been shown to raise the metabolic rate in humans.

Guarana

A plant native to Brazil that has a stimulant power similar to caffeine but with the extra antioxidant benefits of the plant, the Guarana plant has been used for health and bronchi issues.

Lycopene

Tomatoes are another example of vegetables with powerful health-promoting ability.

The active component in tomatoes has been found to be *lycopene*. When consumed in the diet, it has been clinically shown to collect in the prostate tissue in men and the breast tissue in women with protective effects. When I was a kid, tomato ketchup was just ketchup. And if you read the label on any ketchup bottle, it probably talked about how good it tasted on a hotdog or a hamburger.

Today, the marketing has totally changed, and the pitch is all about the power of antioxidants in fruits and vegetables. Pick up any bottle of ketchup now and you will read about the amazing health benefits of lycopene and how it can help protect against cancer.

I am not knocking ketchup, but buyer beware of the commercial pitch as it pertains to your health.

Pycnogenol

A rare tree that grows in the southwestern Bordeaux area of France has a powerful antioxidant in its bark called *pycnogenol,* which has been patented by Horphag Industries. The interesting thing is that pycnogenol has been shown repeatedly in clinical studies to reduce the appearance of varicose veins. How this mystery of nature was unlocked is unknown. Today, you don't have to travel to France and chew on tree bark to get the powerful benefits of pycnogenol. You can simply buy this amazing component as a supplement at your local health food/supplement store. The typical amounts consumed range between 50 to 100 mg/day.

Soy

Although soy as a source of nutrition has been criticized in some circles, the soybean has been harvested as a major macronutrient in the United States and worldwide. The native soybean itself has many interesting properties. On the plus side, the soybean is a plant-based form of a complete protein. That means that the soybean covers all the essential amino acids. Clinical studies have shown that 25 grams of soy in the daily diet can help lower cholesterol. Another plus is that soy is a source of protein.

On the con side, the soybean has antinutrients that have been shown to strip the body of its vitamins and minerals. To fix this issue of antinutrients in the soybean, many companies take out the bad stuff and leave in the good stuff. This makes soy a healthy source of protein, with cholesterol-lowering properties, without the antinutritive effects.

For many years the myth has been purported that soy has an estrogenic effect on the body. Many male athletes that I have spoken with feel it will cause breast development, that they'll be more in touch with their feminine side, and so on. I hear this all the time, and much of the print and Internet media supports this notion.

Another major criticism from athletes is soy's biological value, which is not as high as milk and egg protein. The biological value is a measure of how much protein you actually eat that gets into the muscle tissue. And although soy is not as high as egg, beef, or milk, it does have the beneficial effect of lowering cholesterol.

I generally recommend soy to anyone interested in having a balanced diet. If people choose to be vegetarian, that's fine for philosophical reasons. But, remember, for thousands of years, humans have been eating both animals and plants. This is also supported by our anatomy and physiology.

Soy comes in different forms, including tofu and edamame. Many companies prepare soy burgers or soy dogs, which are soy substitutes with low fat, low calories, and healthy protein.

Soybeans have phytoestrogens; the two best known are genistein and daidzein, both of which have been shown to be protective in prostate tissue and breast tissue. Many researchers have looked at the possible protective effects of these components in cancer cells in these respective tissues.

Soy is an easy way to get some protein in the diet, lower the cholesterol, and protect the cells. The recommended amount is approximately 25 grams per day at least in the daily diet.

VARIETY

The best way to get your nutrients from plants is just that, eat your daily plants: your fruits and vegetables. Another nutritional milestone pioneered at UCLA in David Heber's group is that variety with fruits and vegetables contributes to a wide variety of these beneficial plant nutrients. The wider variety of phytonutrients in the body, the more tools in the body's tool belt to protect against illness.

EAT HEALTHY FAT EVERY DAY

The benefits of fats really come from their structure. A saturated fat by definition means solid at room temperature, like butter or lard. When you think of saturated fat, think about butter. If you take a stick of butter out of the refrigerator and place it on the table, it will remain in a stable form for days. This is because of its chemical structure, which does not allow a breakdown of the components. It is stable, so it does not get oxidized as quickly.

FATS IN THE DIET

An unsaturated fat is by definition liquid at room temperature, like fish oil, olive oil, or flaxseed oil. These forms are easily broken down in structure, which means they can go rancid quickly. When you think of unsaturated, think fish. After you've placed the butter on the table, you could take out some fresh fish and leave it for several days. The difference will be quite dramatic, as the fish will go rancid quickly. The instability of the fish oil causes this rancid state to occur. Anyone who has smelled rotten fish understands the instability of unsaturated fats.

Do we need fat? Yes, we certainly require a minimum amount of fat in the diet.

THE GOOD AND BAD FATS— OMEGA 3s AND OMEGA 6s

Of the many types of fatty acids, two that seem to be making all the headlines these days are the omega 3s and the omega 6s. These names simply describe the chemical structure of fats, but you only need to remember the omega 3s tend to reduce inflammation in the body while the omega 6s tend to promote inflammation in the body. This is the most basic way to describe these two fatty acids. The omega 3s are found in fish, flaxseed, and borage oil, while the omega 6s are found in corn and wheat. Nutritional anthropologists believe that the diet of ancient women and men was relatively balanced between these two fats. Both are important, and a healthy ratio between the two determines health. The omega 3s are also found in ocean plants like seaweed algae.

The fish eat the omega 3–rich algae, the fish store the healthy fats, we eat the fish, and we store the healthy fats. Again, the phrase "you are what you eat" could never be more factual. The omega 3s are also found in grass, which many animals naturally graze on. Cows naturally eat the grass in the fields as they graze, they store the good fats, and we in turn get beef that is high in the good fats.

The change in the food supply has dramatically changed this process. Now, most cows in the United States are corn fed to fatten them up faster for food production. This process is not what nature intended. So once again, we find a disruption of nature's delicate balance.

FIND THE FREE RANGE BEEF

Although the beef that is consumed in many countries today has not been purely free range, Argentina continues to remain a bastion of free-range beef production. The cows are allowed to naturally graze the countryside and feast on the omega 3–rich grass and plants. The meat from these cows is considerably higher in the good fats. Now the consumer is aware and willing to pay. Just recently, the demand for beef in Argentina has been so high that the country has limited export of this prime commodity. It appears that there is a slow turning of the tide toward more natural food supplies. Moreover, the consumer is willing to pay a premium price for these foods. This is a huge step in the right direction, as the food companies respond to consumer desires. If people are willing to pay more money for grass-fed beef, you can bet that farms worldwide will begin to grass-feed more of their cows.

Find the Balance of 3/6

So foods that were typically high in omega 3 good fats have shifted their composition because of manmade practices, which have disturbed the delicate balance that nature created. Whether its beef or fish, stick to what is natural whenever possible. That means looking for the words *free range* and *wild* for beef and fish and avoiding the words *corn fed* and *farm raised*. Remember the ratio; it's not that omega 6s are bad, it's just that our ratio of 3/6 is completely out of control with a huge tilt toward 6.

When we consider all of the breads, chips, crackers, pastas, vegetable oils, wheat products, and corn products we consume as a society, the ratio is ridiculous. Many public health advocates blame this disturbed ratio for the significant increase in the number of chronic diseases that are related to inflammation, such as diabetes, arthritis, cardiovascular disease, asthma, and hyperactivity. Time will tell how related these conditions are to diet, but current research seems to indicate there is a strong correlation. Because the current supply is so heavily tilted toward the omega 6s, the diet has become pro-inflammatory. The ratio has changed dramatically and we are seeing the health consequences.

BEWARE OF THE TRANS FATS

The many types of cholesterol make up an integral component of the body's cells, including skin and hair. So often individuals on extremely low-fat diets will report skin or hair problems. The amazing thing about fats is that just as the bad fats can cause major problems at the cellular level, so can the good fats bring major benefits. This has been evident in the recent research on trans fats, which have been shown to "clog up" the cellular machinery, promoting problems such as heart disease. Trans fats are now widely recognized as a public health menace, and now many cities, such as New York, are planning, or have enacted, laws to ban them in restaurants. The good fats like the omega 3 fats from fish oil have turned out to be almost miraculous. The benefit of these nutrients comes down to processes going on at the cellular level. The bad trans fats are rigid and basically are monkey wrenches thrown into the metabolic engines of cells. As the adage "you are what you eat" has rung true for years, it could not be better represented in this situation. The bad fats screw everything up, while the good fats make the cells healthier. Case in point: The Inuit in Greenland, who have been studied extensively, consume diets very high in omega 3 fats, proven protective for many chronic conditions. The Inuit tend to have much lower incidence rates of stroke, heart attacks, and overall cardiovascular disease. The statistics are quite amazing, and they all boil down to the composition of the diet, in particular, massive amounts of omega 3 fats they consume.

It's been discovered that these good fats tend to be more flexible, which when incorporated into the body's cells, make the cells better at doing their duties. Think of all of your cells as tiny little engines. The engines with good fats are well oiled and running well, while the engines with bad fats have cogs in their machinery, disturbing their delicate balance.

This is the basis behind the good and bad fats and how they affect our bodies at the cellular level.

THE MARKET IS RESPONDING

With the education put forth on the benefits of good fats, the market has responded. Worldwide sales of omega 3–rich fish oil have significantly increased over the last several years. In 2006, sales were up 13 percent over the previous year, most likely in response to the general public wanting more good fats in the diet.

Because of the mercury in the fish, many have advocated limiting the amount served at the dinner table to twice weekly. New studies may be showing that the benefits of the good fats may even outweigh the dangers of mercury toxicity. Even still, most consumers are finding it easier to just take fish-oil tablets, which are often vacuum packed in a process called microencapsulation. This process ensures a long shelf life of this inherently unstable oil. Many consumers prefer having the good old formula of the tablespoon that Mom used to give the kids. The liquid form of fish oil has fewer additives since there are no capsules to ingest, but the bottles have less of a shelf life because of the frequent exposure the oils get to air every time the bottle is opened for use. As long as it is refrigerated, it stays fresh for upward of three to

---

"FISH BURPS"

Many of my patients tell me that they prefer not to take fish oil because of the unpleasant "fish burps" that repeat on them after ingestion.

A nifty trick is to keep the fish-oil tablets/soft gels in the freezer. Take them frozen and you will see this problem quickly disappear. It works every time.

---

four weeks. I highly recommend that all my patients take these as an integral part of the diet.

FISH IS BRAIN FOOD

For years, fish has been called *brain food* and many researchers believe the human brain started to grow significantly when our ancestors began eating fish.

If you look on any label of omega 3–rich oil, fish or flaxseed, you will notice the letters EPA and DHA, eicosanopentanoic acid and docosohexanoic acid respectively. The important point is that the human brain is made up of the DHA component, which is why the "brain" label was tagged on fish. The more we learn about whole foods and the human body, the more we realize the genius of Mother Nature.

Whenever you are at a restaurant, be sure to ask for wild-caught fish, not farm fed. This is -important since many restaurants save money by purchasing farm-fed fish. Farm-feeding is a process in which large amounts of fish are grown and harvested for human consumption, but whenever we disturb the delicate balance of nature, it tends to come back on us. It turns out that farm-fed fish tend to have reduced amounts of the good omega

3 fats and increased amounts of the pro-inflammatory omega 6 fats. This ratio of omega 3 to 6 is disturbed in the fish because they are fed pellets high in the omega 6 inflammatory fats.

Be sure to avoid trans fats whenever possible, although they are hidden in the prepackaged foods we eat. Some countries require reporting the amounts of trans fats on the labels. Often they are hidden as partially hydrogenated vegetable oils, so be sure to check for those key words. Remember, your body is a very complex machine, and we only get one engine, so don't mess up the machinery with trans fats. Instead, get the good fats into your system. As long as you're consuming the correct fats, you can rest assured that they are being incorporated into your body at the cellular level.

FIND HEALTHY
ENERGY SOURCES

HEALTHY ENERGY

I remember a fellow student in medical school who would sip on a two-liter bottle of soda every morning to wake up through morning lectures. His argument was that coffee was too heavily caffeinated, and that he preferred to get two liters of fluid with his super dose of caffeine. I don't see many of my colleagues doing this with soda, but everyone in the hospital has coffee. The more I travel, the more coffeehouses I see.

Recently I had the opportunity to visit the Great Wall and the Forbidden City, both in Beijing, China. At both locations, I noticed brand-new coffeehouses serving sugary lattes and steamy cappuccinos.

Why do we line up at coffeehouses worldwide for the morning latte or espresso? It's because we are constantly looking for energy in this ever-challenging world we live in. Also consider the "energy drink" market, which has expanded to an eight-billion dollar market and is still growing. Not to mention the continued market penetration of sugar-filled sodas all around the world, especially in developing countries. The amazing thing is that these drinks are nothing but water, sugar, and lots of stimulants, with very few nutritious ingredients. They are simply designed to taste good, which means lots of sugars and/or fats, very little protein, vitamins, minerals, and fiber. These are the liquid calories often hidden in the diet that we do not and cannot report. Moreover these hidden calories contribute to the worldwide problem of obesity in both adults and children. The vast majority of consumers are unaware of the high calories in these drinks. These are the hidden calories that I help my patients to realize. There are many lattes that have upward of 500, 600, even 800 calories per serving! Think back to our 2,000-calorie/day recommendation. With two lattes in the morning, consumers have almost satisfied their daily caloric requirement, without even eating any food! What's more, children are now consuming more and more sodas every year as the availability of colas increases worldwide.

THE ENERGY DRINK

Coffee and soda appear to be growing in their respective market shares, but a neighbor has moved in. Now the new energy drink has been born: the "energy drink," which I put in quotes because it's really a misnomer. The explosion of energy drinks started relatively recently and a handful of companies led the charge and have most of the market share. Now, the market has expanded to a multibillion-dollar powerhouse, and it continues to grow.

The typical composition of an energy drink is water, sugar, and caffeine . . . just like a soda. But the difference is the addition of specific nutrients like B vitamins, amino acids like taurine, and antioxidants, which are naturally found in plants. The consumer has responded in a very positive way to these drinks. Whether it's the early morning or late afternoon, people are guzzling from these brightly colored attractive aluminum cans or designer bottles with fancy names that connote energy, vitality, and performance.

I am all for antioxidants, nutrients, and energy. But at what expense? The trade-off for getting some vitamin C and key minerals is having a drink packed with 200 calories of sugar and 150 mg of caffeine. A typical cup of American coffee or an espresso has approximately 100 mg of caffeine.

With the obesity pandemic growing worldwide, every calorie counts, and these drinks are not a solution. If there were more protein, more nutrients packed into these drinks, there could be some justification for all the sugar and caffeine, but unfortunately there is not.

So what to drink when your energy is low? I always first recommend spreading the calories throughout the day in frequent meals and snacks high in protein and low in sugar and fats to maintain a healthy energy level all day. Unfortunately, this is difficult in this day and age with hectic schedules, frequent meetings, family issues, bills, school activities, and so forth. So what's the alternative? I recommend finding healthy sources of energy that are low in calories and high in antioxidants.

My first recommendation: Reach for green tea in the morning instead of that latte or cappuccino. Green tea is probably the best example because it is widely available and easy to prepare. The health benefits have been touted for centuries by the Chinese. When we look at cultures who consumer healthy amounts of green tea, they tend to have healthier profiles. One can buy green tea caffeinated or decaffeinated, but the antioxidant benefits are equal. Unless one adds a large amount of sugar, there are no calories in green tea. Commercially prepared powders are widely available, easy to use hot or cold, and delicious to drink.

There are news reports about the health benefits of red tea from Africa, or white tea, which both may have higher antioxidants per cup than green tea. If that's your choice, great! Just remember, it may not be commercially available worldwide yet. The major benefit of these powerful nutrient-dense drinks compared to coffee, soda, and energy drinks is the calorie control. Remember the first basic point that is paramount in any diet: control the calories.

There are other natural stimulants that are very similar to caffeine. One is guarana, a plant native to Brazil, that is antioxidant rich and has the same naturally stimulating properties of caffeine, while it provides more plant-based nutrients. In fact, just about every popular energy drink on the market has guarana in it for this reason. If you find yourself in Brazil, pure juice from Guarana is very popular. It's the national soft drink, just as popular as the major soda beverages. Make sure if you have guarana, you check the amount of calories, since companies add large amounts of high-calorie sweetener. This defeats the purpose of having the guarana over the other drinks, so be aware.

There are other nutrients that have been suggested to give energy, but time and time again, caffeine continues to prove in clinical studies that it increases energy production in the body by helping to burn more fat and conserve sugars in the muscle tissue. It's no wonder we feel so good after an espresso or a massive latte at the local coffeehouse.

WHEN SUGAR GOES UP, IT MUST COME DOWN

The Spike and the Crash

Have you ever noticed that late afternoon energy starts to drop? Everybody knows that feeling after a heavy carb-laden lunch. You're busy doing your job, and suddenly you have the urge to sleep at your workplace. Then you start to wonder why you could be so sleepy when you got seven hours of sleep. This early afternoon fatigue has little to do with sleep. It is directly related to the diet. So what do we do? The typical action is to wolf down a candy bar, chips, or a sugary snack, then chase it with a strong cup of coffee. Or maybe you just have an energy drink. As pointed out, the spike in energy is great. For a short amount of time, you feel as though you can think clearer, you have more physical energy, and your appetite is relatively curbed. Then comes the drop. Suddenly, you can't function, you can't think straight, you're falling asleep at work or even worse, during a meeting, and you don't know why. It's the inevitable drop-off from the spike that sugar gave you. The caffeine runs its course giving more energy.

The problem is that large amounts of sugar in so many of these snacks causes a spike in blood sugar. When blood sugar goes up, it must come down. The body's response to high sugar is to send out a bunch of insulin into the blood to help reduce the amount of sugar. When insulin lowers blood sugar, then we feel that "low blood sugar" feeling. Often my patients will tell me that they have hypoglycemia (low blood sugar), which usually means that they are snacking during the day, causing these major fluctuations.

So be aware of the spike and the crash. When patients who are following healthy diets come into my office and tell me that they have lost weight and that their energy has gone through the roof, these are the best words I hear in clinic. If a patient reports to me: "The diet program is not working." This simply means that they are eating high-calorie foods in addition to the diet. They have not cut out those hidden calories, and they are probably going over the 2,000-calorie limit.

Conversely, it a patient reports: "I've lost weight and my energy is going through the roof," it means two things.

1. "I've lost weight" means that they've been following the diet plan to control their calories.

2. "My energy is through the roof" means that they've cut out the high-sugar foods that cause the spikes and drops throughout the day. Now they report feeling better at work, in school, or at home performing their daily activities. I always tell my patients that this is the way nature intended for them to feel! It's almost like a natural high.

When you are on the correct eating plan and supporting the diet with natural forms of energy like green tea, then you wonder why you ever ate the way you did in the past. Moreover, you'll never want to go back to feeling that sluggish, tired, low-energy feeling that is so typical of the Western diet.

This problem is running rampant in schools worldwide. Children and young adults are filling themselves up with sugar void of nutrients, causing these fluctuations throughout the day. This problem is so easily cured with proper diet technique, which is simply cutting the sugar and having foods with protein, fiber, antioxidants, vitamins, and minerals.

PREVENT/REVERSE DISEASE WITH GOOD NUTRITION

I wanted to capture everyone's attention in the introduction by pointing out the number of overweight humans worldwide: 1.6 billion. This is the most recently recorded number from the World Health Organization (WHO), however, it is most likely closer to two billion people and increasing daily. One of the most frightening things about this number is the connection to disease. Because overweight and obesity are linked to a spectrum of diseases, doctors around the world are concerned about what lies ahead. We live in a new era of disease. Years ago, humans suffered from infectious diseases, but not the chronic diseases we have today, infections present in different forms, such as bacteria or viruses.

With the worldwide revolution in medicine, we now have good control over most infectious diseases. Because of the growing problem of obesity, most societies are not prepared for the associated chronic diseases. Every area of medicine is affected by this growing problem. The good news is that with good nutrition and proper exercise, this problem is both preventable and reversible.

KIDS WITH AN ADULT DISEASE

For the first time in history, we are seeing chronic health conditions, or lifestyle diseases, in young people. Never before have we seen adult onset diseases in children, all because of too many empty calories in the diet. As children consume these nutrient-poor calories, they accumulate over time and can have a deadly impact. We are only beginning to see the problem on the horizon.

Historically, poor, underdeveloped countries did not face these nutritional problems associated with caloric excess. Generally the nutrition problems seen in those countries were starvation and malnutrition. This was of course due to lack of resources. Now, with even poor children consuming inexpensive foods packed with sugar and fats, we are seeing similar nutritional problems in both ends of the spectrum. In most countries, both developed and developing, we are seeing young people with problems.

THE MUFFIN TOP

People ask me how I know that kids are getting fatter. Well, the statistics continue to show trends toward children who are becoming more obese. But I always say, just look around. I have never seen so many children who are overweight. The best example of this in young people is the "muffin top." When a muffin is baked in the oven, the top expands over the base, creating a mushroom-shaped top.

This description of "muffin top" is now being given to young people who store extra fat in their abdominal section, a new phenomenon that I never encountered growing up. Remember, the more calories we eat, the more calories we store, as seen in "muffin-top" kids.

Although this "muffin top" may sound insignificant, I believe it's important on two levels. One is the obvious risk to children of having extra fat weight in the body, especially in the abdominal section, which is a major risk factor for many diseases. The second issue with the "muffin top" is social acceptance of these children. Many young people I notice out in the streets seem to be proud of this body shape. Where youngsers used to cover up weight around the waist, now they flaunt it. It's almost as though society is giving up on the fight against poor nutrition.

DIABETES IN ADULTS

In the hospital clinic, when we follow the progression of diabetes, the typical patients are older, overweight individuals. We generally diagnose them first with a high blood sugar level and start them on medication, which only serves as a band-aid over a deep laceration. As we follow these patients, their diabetes generally gets worse for several reasons.

One, because most doctors don't learn much about nutrition in medical school (nutrition is not considered an important part of the curriculum), they simply do not perform appropriate nutritional counseling.

Moreover, even if doctors do have extensive knowledge in the area of nutrition, they do not have time to do the proper workup on the patient.

So we have millions of diabetic patients worldwide being treated with a variety of medications that only address their symptoms, not the root cause of the disease. As a result, the patients accumulate more weight, get on more medications, and tend to get more severe symptoms.

Then comes the bad stuff.

WHEN DIABETES TAKES ITS TOLL

Diabetics, over time, are at very high risk for

- Loss of vision
- Heart attacks
- Strokes
- Kidney problems leading to dialysis
- Poor circulation leading to amputation

Now as bad as that sounds, imagine the same thing happening to a young child. Instead of the these problems starting around 60 years of age, now we are beginning to see them in young teenagers of 13 or 14 years. This means by the age of 30, many of these young folks will be blind, will have had a heart attack and/or a stroke, be on dialysis, and possibly have an amputated limb. All because of the diet. This is an entirely preventable disease when it comes to nutrition, but the diet in today's children worldwide is only getting worse.

YOU'VE HEARD IT BEFORE: DIET AND EXERCISE

All of these horrible events from a poor diet? The answer is yes. The vast majority of these problems today are preventable with a good diet and exercise. How many times have you heard diet and exercise. I firmly believe most people know what they need to do, but they don't know how to do it. There are so many different diet programs and exercise routines, but my goal in writing this book was to provide something useful for the average person concerned with their health.

Addressing the two issues of high calorie intake and low physical activity is paramount. As a physician and an educator, it's very important to stress that the calories being consumed is a major culprit in this worldwide crime against humanity. In addition, a major part of this book is dedicated to educating people on how to exercise and maintain a healthy level of physical activity.

Many have blamed the Internet, video games, and lack of recess for the current rise in obesity in kids. Although those elements do factor in, the lion's share of blame rests on the calorically dense, prepackaged food that we as a global society are voraciously consuming. Unless we slow this runaway train, the medical problems associated with obesity that will run rampant in the near future will prove devastating.

PART TWO

EXERCISE

CHAPTER 8

THE IMPORTANCE OF MUSCLE

hy is muscle so important for us? Consider again our forbearers' philosophy of activity. They hunted, gathered, and protected in their respective environments, which was a good way for them to use their muscles. When the long winters came, muscle was expendable and was most likely the first tissue they lost.

MADONNA BODY

Consider the engine analogy with your body muscle. If you have a bigger engine burning more fuel as calories, then you may run through too much energy when you need those very calories for storage. It's important to realize how important muscle is. I often tell my patients no matter what age they are, to pursue a body with healthy muscle. In fact, I often use the singer Madonna as the gold standard of what healthy muscle tissue looks like. Madonna, who is approaching a very youthful 50 and look at her anatomy. In the past ages, women most likely had similar builds, a healthy amount of muscle mass and very little fat on the body— long, slender muscles, toned and separated. The small amount of fat men and women did have was for survival. To make it through those long winters, it was important to cut down the size of the engine so as to not burn too many calories. Today, where we have plentiful food and fast food around every corner, it's much more important to preserve our lean muscle mass in the body to ensure a healthy metabolism. As mentioned earlier, there is no animal species that gains muscle as they age. We humans see a significant loss of muscle over time, which is one of the most important reasons for disability. Both men and women peak [copy missing?]

MUSCLE MASS AND AGING

New research suggests that muscle may improve quality of life and may in fact extend life. As we age, we naturally lose muscle. Every ten years, we lose 3 percent of our total muscle mass starting around the age of 30. This is one reason why you'll hear people worldwide claiming that after 30, it's all downhill. Things are drooping, loose, and soft. When you think about it, there is no animal that grows older and grows more muscle mass as a normal process of aging. Could you imagine how big your typical 85-year-old would be? Again, Mother Nature kicked this process into play. As we age and lose muscle, it's an efficient way to make sure we are not burning too many calories.

As stated earlier, our body's muscles are the engines in cars. A large truck requires an enormous amount of gasoline to fuel its big engine, while a fuel-efficient mini-car requires very little gasoline. This is the same principle of the body's muscle. More muscle requires more calories, so a big football player may need more fuel (4,000 calories) to perform his daily activities well, while an 85-year-old woman with very little muscle may only need a few (1,000 calories). It's all about the muscle. Muscle is a living breathing tissue just like all of the body's organ systems. So think car engine when you think about muscle, and it's generally better to have a bigger engine than a smaller one as we age. Not only does more muscle help with burning calories, it also helps with balance and performing our activities of daily living (ADLs). Some preeminent researchers in aging have tapped into the benefits of building muscle even at an advanced age. Dr. Bill Evans, at the University of Arkansas, has done just that.

In clinical trials, he was able to prove that older people, who performed resistance training were able to build muscle and improve their functional capacity. Muscle helps to foster independence in older individuals, which is why I consider it the most important antiaging tissue in the body.

So remember to eat sufficient protein in the diet, maintain a healthy muscle mass, and of course stay active (which we'll discuss in later chapters).

TOO MUCH MUSCLE?

There is of course a limit to muscle being beneficial. Athletes who use steroids are good example of pushing the limits. When there is too much muscle in the body, the heart and other vital organs have difficulty supporting it. It's as if an engine was too big and uncontrollable. It would eventually burn out the system. So healthy muscle is the key to longevity. In his recent book healthy aging, Dr. Andrew Weil points to the inhabitants of Okinawa Japan as having one of the healthiest lifestyles in the world. He points to physical activity being an integral part of the society which is why there are so many 90-year-olds walking around Okinawa looking healthy and happy. So remember the muscle for a variety of reasons, but with weight management, think the size of your engine determines the calories you burn every day.

So use it and don't lose it. Support it with a healthy diet balanced with sufficient physical activity. How do we build healthy muscle tissue? We exercise.

AEROBIC AND RESISTANCE EXERCISE

There are two types of exercise *aerobic* and *resistance*.

1. Aerobic exercise is important for the cardiovascular system. It is defined by repetitive motion such as running, swimming, or cycling. In general, this type of exercise does not build muscle tissue. If you look at any elite endurance athlete, he or she does not carry a large amount of muscle around. These athletes are very thin, with muscle developed only in certain areas. Professional cyclists may have large legs but their upper body musculature is minimal. Marathon runners are usually thin, both upper body and lower body. When I test these athletes in the laboratory at UCLA for example, they tend to have very low cholesterol levels and very low resting heart rates. But too much is not good. Many of these athletes tend to have weak bone health and loss of lean muscle because of the nature of their exercise.

2. At the other end of the spectrum is resistance exercise, which is defined by short bursts of energy. These types of exercise include weight lifting, football, track and field sports, and so forth. Take your typical strength athletes and they will have very healthy muscle and good bone health, but perhaps an unhealthy cholesterol profile and unhealthy cardiovascular system. So the opposite ends of the spectrum can be unhealthy. It's important to consider the happy medium. Incorporating a little of both endurance and strength training into the daily routine is important. I recommend working out for at least 30 minutes three times weekly, although a little more does not hurt. Our ancestors probably never had repetitive joint pain because they did not have

treadmills or squat racks to work out on. These are machines that currently have given many people repetitive injuries. So a little of both is best.

I work out every day but I always rotate my program so that I am challenging my muscles to a different routine. It's a simple way to keep you and your body interested. Avoid boring workouts that have the same routine. Not only will it challenge your muscles in a healthy way to respond, but it will help avoid injury to the joints, bones, and muscles.

CHAPTER NINE

THE SIMPLE 7

So what is the easiest way to work the whole body? Very simply, I developed what I call *The Simple 7*—the seven main muscle groups we work on throughout the week. The Simple 7 includes:

1. Chest
2. Biceps: Front of arms
3. Triceps: Back of arms
4. Abs (can be worked on daily)
5. Back
6. Front of legs
7. Back of legs.

Generally I split a workout between alternating days: The first day I will work upper body, the next day lower body. Again, work abs every day to help strengthen the core.

Doing some healthy cardio means a good 15 minutes of elevated heart rate. There is plenty of evidence to support the notion that 15 minutes of cardio daily has profound impact on heart health.

Don't worry about spending an hour on a treadmill; the added benefit is minimal and may actually work against you.

There are approximately 260 muscles in the body. So why just work on seven, and why these seven? Well it's all about getting the most bang for your effort. When exercising, it's best to work on large muscle groups. It's as if you are fine-tuning a regular car engine as opposed to an engine in a toy boat. The larger the muscle, the more metabolic benefit, and the bigger the payoff when it comes to weight maintenance. The Simple 7 group consists of the fewest number of muscles groups one has to work on to achieve maximum benefit in an exercise routine. You can exercise with more or less, but if you attack these particular muscles, then you will achieve maximum benefit. Also, it's important to realize that the body is a balanced machine, and you must work the lower with the upper and the back with the front. The seven muscle groups provide total balance in an easy way.

HOW OFTEN SHOULD YOU WORK OUT?

How much you work out depends on your schedule, but I recommend three to five times a week. I work out every day, but I incorporate a tremendous amount of variety into my routines for a number of reasons. One reason is to always keep my workouts interesting. Another reason is to move the stress around the body. You don't want to repeat the same exercise over and over again every day, because that will wear on the joints, bones, muscles, tendons, and ligaments.

I generally recommend splitting up the week. For those of you who can only work out three days a week, which I consider the minimum, either rotate Monday, Wednesday, and Friday. Or you can do Tuesday, Thursday, and Saturday. This allows one day in between for rest. This rest time gives the body an opportunity to grow and repair from the damage caused by exercise. Within those three days, you can rotate exercises, so Monday would be upper body and abs, Wednesday, lower body and abs, then Friday upper body and abs again. The following Monday, you could rotate so that Monday is lower body and abs, Wednesday is upper body and abs, and then Friday is lower body and abs again.

This allows that necessary rest time between exercises for optimal muscle health. Three days a week is the basic minimum routine. On each day, the workouts should be split between cardio and resistance: 30 minutes of each is perfect. The cardio exercises should be rotated as well, so that Monday is the treadmill, Wedneday is the bike, and Friday is the elliptical. This again allows variety so that you're not bored, and it spreads the stress around the body's tissues so as to avoid overuse injuries that are so common.

If you prefer to exercise more, then I would recommend five or even six days a week. With more days, you can split up your workouts more. For example, Monday, instead of just doing upper body, you do very specific upper body such as chest and biceps with abs. Remember, abs are done every day to strengthen your core. Then Tuesday you could do specific lower body such as quads, calves, and abs.

Going on to Wednesday, you're back to upper body so that you're doing upper back, triceps, and abs. Thursday, hamstrings and abs. Then Friday you can repeat your Monday workout so that you've come full circle and have given your body ample time to rest. This is the best workout for the individual who does not have time to spend two hours in the gym every day. The cardio exercise should be done after your strength workout. I prefer this for a couple of reasons. Number one, you will not be as tired for your strength training, for which it is more important to be well rested. A second reason is the sweat. After running on a treadmill or stair stepper for 30 minutes, your body's sweat and salts are coming out of your pores, which makes for a more challenging weight workout. The bar may be slipping from your grasp; you'll be sliding around in the machines, and so forth. So try to do weights first, then cardio. The only reason I recommend some people start with cardio is that those individuals are very tight and tell me that their muscles are cold in the morning. For these people, I think cardio beforehand may actually improve their workouts. It tends to make them more limber and gets the blood circulating around the body.

HOW DO MUSCLES GROW?

You are continually placing stress on your body's tissues when you exercise, which is how you attain muscle growth. When you work out, you basically damage muscle tissue. When this tissue gets damaged, it repairs itself and comes back stronger. This is the process behind muscle growth and repair with exercise.

IN THE GYM, THE HOTEL, OR AT HOME

"I Lift Weights and Get Big!"

One of the most common complaints I hear from my female patients is the fear of getting big muscles when they lift weights. Especially, when I recommend a healthy amount of resistance training, the immediate reaction is fear of gaining too much muscle and having manly arms. First off, I tell them it's very difficult for women to build muscle because of their hormonal makeup. Women have less testosterone circulating around the body then men do, so they are already at a disadvantage. Men lift weights, constantly trying to build more muscle, and they are already given the upper hand when it comes to muscle because of their makeup. But even with that advantage, men still purchase hundreds of millions of dollars of supplements to build and maintain more lean muscle mass. Given this, the myth about women is simply wrong. Women should be performing resistance activity throughout the week to challenge that muscle. More muscle means more physical capability and higher metabolism. A higher metabolism means a bigger engine in the car, which helps maintain a healthy weight over time. Maintaining a healthy weight goes both ways.

The new science is a focus on healthy muscle development at any age after 18.

WHY EXERCISE AT ALL?

There are so many benefits to exercise, and every day, we are discovering new ones.

A recent *Newsweek* article discussed how exercise can boost brain power and fight off diseases like Alzheimer's—more incredible information in an already long list of benefits. New research in animal models has shown that exercise stimulates a hormone called IGF-1, or insulin such as growth factor-1, which in turn goes to the brain to stimulate another called *brain-derived neurotrophic factor* (BDNF). BDNF is believed to facilitate a process in which an animal's brain nerve cells branch out and communicate with each other. In fact, research has supported that theory that a brain with lower levels of BDNF is challenged with retaining new information. How amazing is exercise—not only does it build the body, but the mind as well! Exercise not only slows the aging process in the brain, but reverses it. Research has also shown that active adults have less inflammation in the brain and fewer transient ischemic attacks, or ministrokes, which can impair cognition. People who exercise regularly tend to have higher levels of the neurotransmitters that regulate mood, such as serotonin, dopamine, and norepinephrine. With so many people on psychotropic medication, exercise is proving to be an inexpensive method of maintaining mental health. As with the body's muscle mass, the same holds true for the brain: use it or lose it. Within just a short month of stopping physical activity, the new brain tissue connections that were formed basically shrink down back to normal.

Many parents of children with attention deficit/hyperactivity disorder (ADHD) already know the benefits of physical activity on their children. It tends to help regulate their moods. An exercise prescription can often be given in conjunction with medication for these ADHD children\or may even replace a medication regimen.

This has broad-ranging implications for children in school and their curriculum. With so many schools having downsized the number of physical education classes with a focus on more class time, this could be detrimental. That extra time on the playground may actually boost test scores in all children. The great thing about introducing physical education at an early age in school is that it sets the tone for future exercise. Once a healthy habit like exercise is established, it tends to carry on. When people understand the importance, it becomes even more of a regular routine

So we know the benefits of exercise for all types of health. Not only does exercise help with all chronic conditions, it also promotes wellness. Following , you will notice a variety of exercises that will help to support a healthy active lifestyle.

EXERCISE

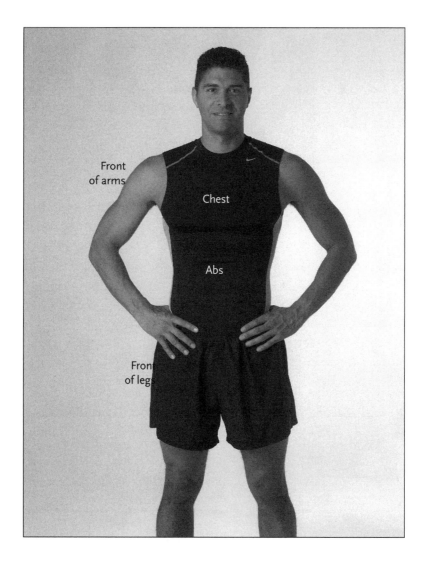

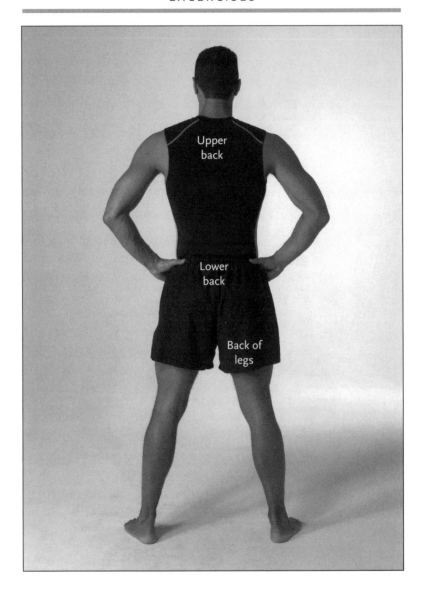

STRETCHES BEFORE EXERCISING

Following is a series of 7 simple stretches:

#1. Side Stretch

Starting from standing position, simply lean to one side and hold. Alternate, and perform stretch on other side.

#2. Squat and Turn Stretch

In squatting position, slowly reach out to one side, rotating torso. Alternate, perform stretch on other side.

#3. Tricep and Back Stretch

In standing position, hold arm at elbow and pull toward face for stretch across back and arm. Alternate, perform stretch on other side.

#4. Calf/Leg Stretch

In standing position, slowly lean forward with heel on ground until stretch is felt, then hold. Alternate, perform stretch on other side.

#5. Thigh/Groin Stretch

In sitting position with feet touching, slowly lean elbows on legs until stretch in groin area is felt.

#6. Hurdler Stretch

Pull one leg back, and lean forward toward toes. Alternate, perform stretch on other side.

#7. Stretch with Back Curled

On back, bring knees to chest and hold.

#1. Side Stretch

Starting from standing position, simply lean to one side and hold. Alternate, and perform stretch on other side.

#2. Squat and Turn Stretch

In squatting position, slowly reach out to one side, rotating torso. Alternate, perform stretch on other side.

#3. Tricep and Back Stretch

In standing position, hold arm at elbow and pull toward face for stretch across back and arm. Alternate, perform stretch on other side.

#4. Calf/Leg Stretch

In standing position, slowly lean forward with heel on ground until stretch is felt, then hold. Alternate, perform stretch on other side.

#5. Thigh/Groin Stretch

In sitting position with feet touching, slowly lean elbows on legs until stretch in groin area is felt.

#6. Hurdler Stretch

Pull one leg back, and lean forward toward toes. Alternate, perform stretch on other side.

#7. Stretch with Back Curled

On back, bring knees to chest and hold.

#1. CHEST

Dumbbell Bench Press

Dumbbell Bench Press with Legs Up

Dumbbell Fly

Dumbbell Bench Press

A. Hold dumbbells and lie down on bench with your feet on the ground.

B. Slowly bring dumbbells down to side of the body.

C. Bring dumbbells down toward the chest and push up to
starting position

Dumbbell Bench Press with Legs Up

A. To challenge the core-stabilizing muscles more, raise the legs while keeping the back flat. Perform the same dumbbell press.

B. Lower dumbbells down toward chest.

C. When dumbbells reach chest, slowly return to starting position.

Dumbbell Fly

A. Hold dumbbells and lie down on bench with feet on ground.

B. Lower dumbbells to the sides, maintaining an angle at the elbow joint.

C. Bring dumbbells back up to starting position, holding angle in elbow.

Dumbbell Fly with Legs Up

To challenge the core muscle more, raise legs while keeping back flat. Perform the same dumbbell fly exercise.

Hold dumbbells and lie down on bench with feet in the air.

Lower dumbbells to the sides, maintaining an angle at the elbow joint.

Bring dumbbells back up to starting position, holding angle in elbow.

Push Ups

When traveling or when at home, with no access to a gym, simple pushups can be easily performed.

A. Place palms on ground approximately shoulder length apart and lock elbows in starting position.

B. Slowly lower body toward the ground while looking straight ahead. Do not allow your face or chest to touch the ground.

C. Push up to return to starting position. Try not to lock
    arms in between repetitions.

#2. BICEPS

Standing Bicep Curls: One Arm at a Time
Alternate Arm Bicep Curl
Standing Bicep Curl: Both Arms at the Same Time
Standing Bicep Curl: Both Arms at Home
Standing Bicep Curl: At Home /Alternate Arm
Standing Bicep Curl: Traveling

Standing Bicep Curls: One Arm at a Time

A. In standing position, hold dumbbells by side of the body.

B. In slow, controlled movements, bend at the elbow and raise arm up. Only working one side of the body. Repeat with the alternate arm.

C. Perform 10 repetitions, 3 sets each for a total of 30.

Alternate Arm Bicep Curl

Perform 10 repetitions, 3 sets each for a total of 30 for each arm

A. In standing position, hold dumbbells by side of the body.

B. In slow controlled movements, bend at the elbow and raise arm up, working on one side of body, then alternate to other hand.

Standing Bicep Curl: Both Arms at the Same Time

Perform 3 sets of 10 reps for a total of 30

A. In standing position, hold both dumbbells at your side

B. Bend both elbows at the same time, raising both hands up toward the face.

C. After raising dumbbells to shoulders, return both hands to
   starting position, repeating movement 10 times.

Standing Bicep Curl: At Home

At home, substitute dumbbell with empty liquid laundry detergent container with comfortable handle. Add water to container to increase weight resistance. Repeat the same activity. Perform 10 repetitions, 3 sets each for a total of 30.

A. In standing position, take container and hold it by side of the body.

B. In slow controlled movements, bend at the elbow and raise arm up, only working on one side of the body.

Standing Bicep Curl: At Home/Alternate Arm

In standing position, take container and hold it by side of the body. In slow controlled movements, bend at the elbow and raise arm up, working on one side of body, then alternate to other side. Perform 3 sets of 10 repetitions

Standing Bicep Curl: Traveling

When traveling with no access to gym nor equipment, use a water bottle with a comfortable grip. Fill with water for comfortable level of resistance during activity. Perform same activity as described with dumbbells or detergent containers. Perform 10 repetitions, 3 sets each for a total of 30.

#3. TRICEPS

Kick Backs

Tricep Kick Backs Alternate Arm

Overhead Tricep Press

Overhead Tricep Press: Back View

Dips for Triceps

Kick Backs

Perform 3 sets for a total of 30 repetitions.

A. Hold one dumbbell at a time, in position standing and leaning forward

B. Hold arm with upper arm against side of the body

C. Push dumbbell toward your back exending at the elbow, return to original position, and repeat 10 times.

Tricep Kick Backs Alternate Arm

When changing to the alternate arm, move your leg back to stabilize.

A. Hold dumbbell in alternate hand by the side in standing position

B. Slowly push back dumbbell.

C. Extend elbow back, and slowly return to starting position.

Overhead Tricep Press

Perform 3 sets of 10 repetitions for a total of 30.

A. With both hands, grab dumbbell behind head, starting in a neutral position.

B. In slow, controlled movements, press dumbbell over the head until elbows are almost locked.

C. Slowly return to resting position, and repeat for a total of 10 repetitions.

Overhead Triceps Press: Back View

Same exercise but with back view. Look straight ahead, do not
strain neck in an uncomfortable position.

A. With both hands, grab dumbbell behind the head, starting
   in a neutral position. Perform 3 sets of 10 repetitions for a
   total of 30.

B. In slow, controlled movements, press dumbbell ahead of head until elbows are almost locked.

C. After full extension, slowly return to resting position, and
repeat for a total of 10 repetitions.

Dips for Triceps

Either when traveling or at home, sit on the edge of a chair and slowly perform dip, keeping the body stabilized.

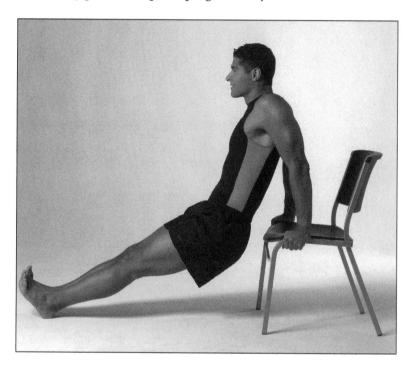

A. Find a dip machine in the gym either sitting or standing positions.

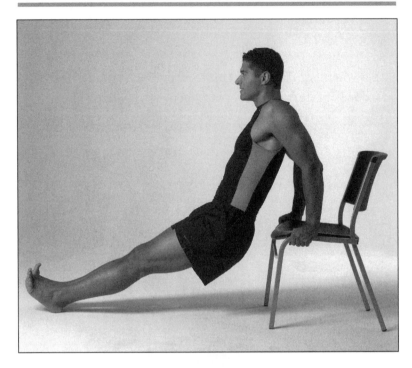

B. From starting position, slowly move into dip
without straining.

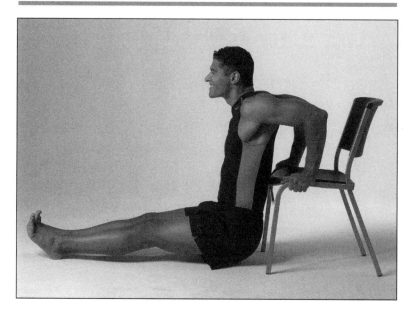

C. Return to neutral position avoiding straining, using slow controlled movement

#4. ABDOMINALS (ABS)

Abs at 60-degree position

Abs at 90-degree position

Abs at 120-degree position

In the gym, at home, or while traveling, lie flat and perform abdominal curl. Gently curl body, lifting head and neck 6 inches off of the ground. Relax hands lightly touching temples. Start with legs in a 60-degree position. Return head to resting position, and avoid straining neck during exercise.

Abs at 90-degree position

Same exercise as the 60-degree position, but in a 90-degree position. Moderate difficulty

In the gym, at home, or while traveling, lie flat and perform abdominal curl. Gently curl body, lifting head and neck 6 inches off of the ground. Relax hands lightly touching temples. Start with legs in 60-degrees position Return head to resting position, and avoid straining neck during exercise.

Abs at 120-degree position

Same exercise in 120-degree position. High level of difficulty. Keep back flat on bench or ground

In the gym, at home, or while traveling, lie flat and perform abdominal curl. Gently curl body, lifting head and neck 6 inches off of the ground. Relax hands lightly touching temples. Start with legs in 60-degree position. Return head to resting position, and avoid straining neck during exercise.

#5. BACK

Dumbbell Rows

Door Towel Pulls

Bent Reverse Flys

Dumbbell Rows

If traveling with no gym access, use a comfortable chair or couch instead of a bench. Perform 3 sets for a total of 30 on each side.

A. Holding one dumbbell in hand, bend over bench with opposite hand resting toward front of bench.

B. Starting position with dumbbell by the side. In a slow, controlled movemen, bring elbow up.

C. Return dumbbell to starting position by the side of the body and repeat 10 times.

Door Towel Pulls

When traveling with no access to gym equipment.

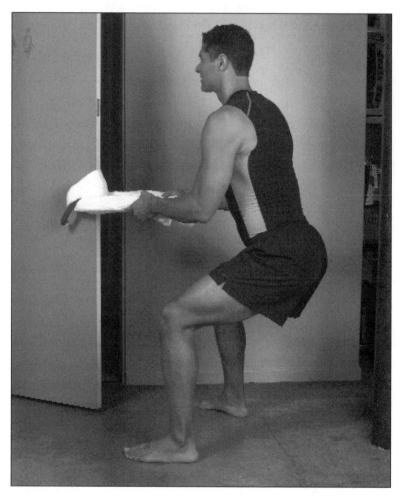

Tie towel around door handle Pull isometric contraction with both arms applying equal pressure. Perform exercise while in squatting position, and hold for 10 seconds. Stand up and relax. Then repeat exercise for a total of 3 times.

Bent Reverse Flys

The exercise can be done without weights if desired. Follow the same instructions. Use dumbbells, water bottles, or detergent containers for additional resistance.

A. Standing in slight squatting position, with back straight.

B. Bring arms up and back.

C. In slow and controlled movement, return to starting position and repeat for a total of 10 repetitions. Perform exercise in 3 sets of 10 reps for a total of 30.

Bent Reverse Flys Focus

The exercise can be done without weights if desired. Follow the same instructions.Perform exercise in 3 sets of 10 reps for a total of 30.

A. Standing in slight squatting position, with back straight.

B. Bring arms up and back.

C. In slow and controlled movement, return to starting position and repeat for a total of 10 repetitions.

#6 LEGS: FRONT

Leg Raise

Dumbbell Squat

Wall Squat

Standing Squat

Leg Raise

These exercises can be done in a gym, at home or while traveling. Perform 10 repetitions each set, and do 3 sets for a total of 30 on each leg.

A. Lie down on bench, with flat back and stabilize the body.

B. From stable neutral position, raise each leg individually while stabilizing the body. Return leg to starting position, then alternate to other leg.

Dumbbell Squat

At home, use detergent containers or water bottles.
While traveling use water bottles and fill with water until
resistance is comfortable.

A. Holding dumbbells in one hand each, start in neutral
position.

B. Slowly squat down, without straining, holding dumbbells on each side.

C. Slowly return to a standing position in a controlled fashion.

Wall Squat

A. With back leaning against a wall, place feet at shoulder width apart.

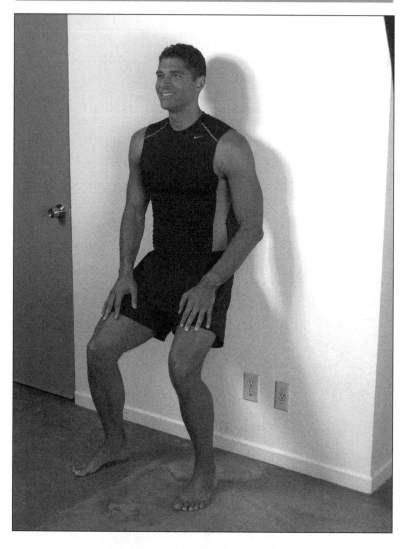

B. Lean back against the wall and slowly go into squat
   position. Hold for 10 seconds.

C. Return to standing position, and repeat for a total of 3 sets.

Standing Squat

These can be done in a gym, at home, or when traveling. Perform a total of 3 sets.

A. With no wall, simply stand in position with your feet shoulder width apart.

B. In a slowly controlled fashion, squat into a comfortable position and hold for 10 seconds.

C. Slowly return to original position, take a brief rest, and repeat.

#7. LEGS: BACK

Leg Kick Backs

Leg Curl on Bench

Leg Kick Backs

There are various machines in the gym which concentrate on the muscles in the back of the legs. If no access to leg curl machine, simply stabilize on bench and perform leg kick backs.

A. In a gym, find machine for leg kick backs. Push back one leg at a time,

B. Return leg to starting position

C. Repeat with opposite leg, doing 10 repetitions for each leg and 3 sets for a total of 30 on each leg

Leg Curl on Bench

These exercises can be done in the gym, at home, or while traveling.

A. Stabilize on bench with thigh held out

B. In slow and controlled motion, curl leg with foot towards
   back

C. Return to original position, and repeat with opposite leg.
Perform 10 repetitions and 3 sets for a total of 30.

7-STEP TOTAL BODY EXERCISE

Finally, if you only have the time and energy to do one exercise, there is one you can do everyday in a slow and controlled motion. Using a pair of dumbbells or water bottles, or other objects for resistance, simply perform the 7 stages of this exercise for a total body workout in just a matter of minutes.

A. Stand in starting position, holding a dumbbell in each hand.

B. Squat down slowly, holding dumbbells by side of the body.

C. Push with legs in slow and controlled motion and return to
   original standing position

D. Raise dumbbells up toward chest area and hold briefly

E. Press dumbells over your head in a slow and controlled movement

F. Slowly bring dumbbells down from overhead position

G. Return dumbbells to side of the body and repeat exercise.
    Perform this exercise in 10 repetitons and in 3 sets for a
    total of 30 reps.

APPENDIX A

FOOD LISTS

PROTEIN FOODS—Calorie Average 140

Food Item	Portion	Calories
Beef, lean cuts	3 oz., cooked	145–60
Chicken, breast preferred	3 oz., cooked	140
Cottage cheese, nonfat	1 cup	140
Eggs	2 eggs	160
Egg whites	7 whites	115
Fish	4 oz., cooked	130–70
Pork, lean cuts	3 oz., cooked	150–65
Protein powder + nonfat milk	1 scoop protein powder + 1 cup nonfat milk	200
Scallops	4 oz., cooked	135
Shrimp, crab, lobster	4 oz., cooked	120
Soy burgers	2 patties	160
Soy "ground round"	3/4 cup	120
Tofu, firm	1/2 cup	180
Tuna, water packed	4 oz.	145
Turkey, breast preferred	3 oz., cooked	135
Yogurt, plain nonfat	1 cup	140

FRUITS—Calorie Average 70

Food Item	Portion	Calories	Fiber (g)
Apricots	3 whole	50	3
Avocado	¼ average fruit	80	2
Banana	1 small	90	3
Blackberries	1 cup	75	8
Blueberries	1 cup	110	5
Cantaloupe	1 cup, cubed	55	1
Grapefruit	½ fruit	40	2
Grapefruit juice	½ cup	50	0
Grapes	1 cup	115	2
Honeydew	1 cup cubed	60	1
Kiwi	1 large	55	3
Mango	½ large	80	3
Nectarine	1 large	70	2
Orange	1 large	85	4
Orange juice	½ cup	50	0
Papaya	½ large	75	3
Peach	1 large	70	3
Pineapple	1 cup, diced	75	2
Plums	2 small	70	2
Prunes	3 whole	60	2
Red apple	1 medium	100	4
Red pear	1 medium	100	4
Strawberries	1 cup, sliced	50	4
Tangerine	1 medium	45	3
Watermelon	1 cup, balled	50	1

VEGETABLES, COOKED—Calorie Average 55

Food Item	Portion	Calories	Fiber (g)
Acorn squash, baked	1 cup	85	6
Artichoke	1 medium	60	6
Asparagus	1 cup	45	4
Beets	1 cup	75	3
Broccoli	1 cup	45	5
Brussels sprouts	1 cup	60	4
Cabbage	1 cup	35	4
Carrots	1 cup	70	5
Cauliflower	1 cup	30	3
Celery	1 cup	20	2
Chinese cabbage	1 cup	20	3
Collard greens	1 cup	50	5
Eggplant	1 cup	30	3
Green beans	1 cup	45	4
Kale	1 cup	35	3
Leeks	1 cup	30	1
Mushrooms	1 cup	40	3
Mustard greens	1 cup	20	3
Onion	1 cup	105	4
Pumpkin	1 cup	50	3
Red cabbage	1 cup	30	3
Spinach	1 cup	40	4
Swiss chard	1 cup	20	2
Tomatoes	1 cup	70	3
Tomato juice	1 cup	40	1
Tomato sauce/puree	1 cup	100	5
Tomato soup, with water	1 cup	85	0
Tomato vegetable juice	1 cup	45	2
Turnip greens	1 cup	30	5
Winter squash	1 cup	70	7
Zucchini with skin	1 cup	30	3

VEGETABLES, RAW—Calorie Average 55

Food Item	Portion	Calories	Fiber (g)
Cabbage	1 cup	20	2
Carrots	1 cup	50	4
Cucumber	1 cup	15	1
Endive	1 cup	10	2
Lettuce, romaine	1 cup	10	1
Pepper, green, chopped	1 cup	30	2
Peppers, red, chopped	1 cup	30	2
Pepper, yellow, chopped	1 cup	30	2
Spinach	1 cup	10	1
Tomatoes, chopped	1 cup	40	2

STARCHES, STARCHY VEGETABLES, AND GRAINS—Calorie Average 100

Food Item	Portion	Calories	Fiber (g)
Beans, black, pinto, etc.	½ cup, cooked	115–140	5–7
Bread, whole grain preferred	1 slice	100	3
Cereal, bran, high fiber	2/3 cup	90–120	15–18
Corn	1 ear, or ½ cup	75	2
Crackers, whole grain Ry-Krisp, Wasa, etc.	4 crackers	100	
English muffin, whole grain preferred	1 muffin	100	5
Lentils	½ cup, cooked	115	8
Oatmeal, cooked in water	1 cup	130	4
Pasta, whole grain preferred	½ cup, cooked	85	2
Peas, green	2/3 cup	95	6
Pita bread, or hamburger bun whole grain preferred	½ pita or ½ burger bun	85	2
Popcorn, air popped	4 cups	100	
Potato, sweet preferred	½ cup	100	2
Rice, brown preferred	½ cup, cooked	110	2
Rice cakes	14 small or 2 large	100	2
Shredded wheat, bite size	1 cup	110	4
Tortillas, corn	2 tortillas	80	
Waffle, whole/multi grain	1 waffle	80	2

EXTRAS—Calorie Average 65

Food Item	Portion	Calories	Fiber (g)
Cheese, Parmesan	3 tbsp	80	5
Cheese, reduced fat	1 oz.	50–80	2–5
Honey, jam, jelly	1 tbsp	50	0
Nuts	1/2 oz.	80–100	6–11
Olive Oil	1 tsp	40	4
Olives	10 large	50	7
Pine nuts, sesame seeds	1 tbsp (40 nuts)	50	4–7
Salad Dressing, fat-free or lowfat	2 tbsp	20–60 (varies)	2–5

PROTEIN SNACKS—Calorie Average 100

Food Item	Portion	Calories	Protein
Cheese, mozzarella, lowfat	1 oz. (1 stick)	70	8
Cottage cheese, nonfat	½ cup	70	14
Milk, nonfat or 1% fat	1 cup	90–110	9
Soup, tomato, made with nonfat milk	1 cup	120	6
Soy crisps	1 oz. (± 20)	110	7
Soy nuts	1 oz.	110	11
Yogurt, nonfat, sugar-free	6-oz. carton	100	5

APPENDIX B

MEAL PLANS

1,200-CALORIE MEAL PLAN

Protein	Fruit	Vegetable	Starch/Grain	Protein Snack	Extras*
3	2	4	2	1	2

Breakfast: 1 protein + 1 fruit
    Examples:
    7 egg whites (hard boiled or omelet cooked with pan spray)
    and 1/2 grapefruit
    or:
    1 cup nonfat cottage cheese and 1 cup pineapple

Lunch: 1 protein + 2 vegetables + salad + 1 starch/grain + 1 extra
    Examples:
    3 oz. roasted chicken breast
    with 4 cups of salad greens + 2 tbsp. of lowfat dressing
    and 2 cups steamed broccoli
    and 2 large multigrain rice cakes
    or:
    4 oz. waterpack tuna on 4 cups greens + 2 tbsp. lowfat dressing
    with 1 cup fresh diced tomatoes
    and 1 cup cucumbers
    and ½ cup cooked black beans

PM Snack: 1 protein snack + 1 fruit
    Examples:
    1 oz. stick mozzarella cheese
    and 1 apple

Dinner: 1 protein + 2 vegetables + salad + 1 starch/grain + 1 extra
    Examples:
    4 oz. broiled fish with teriyaki sauce
    and 1 cup steamed spinach + 1 cup steamed carrots
    and mixed green salad + 2 tbsp lowfat dressing
    and ½ cup sweet potato or ½ cup brown rice

*See "Extras" in Appendix A, page 150, for food items.

1,500-CALORIE MEAL PLAN

Protein	Fruit	Vegetable	Starch/Grain	Protein Snack	Extras*
4	3	4	3	1	2

Breakfast: 1 protein + 1 starch
   Examples:
   7 egg whites (hard boiled or omelet cooked with pan spray)
   with 1/2 grapefruit and 1 slice whole-grain toast
   or:
   1 cup nonfat cottage cheese, 1 cup pineapple, and 1 English muffin

Lunch: 1 protein + 2 vegetables + salad + 1 starch/grain + 1 extra
   Examples:
   3 oz. roasted chicken breast
   with 4 cups of salad greens + 2 tbsp. of lowfat dressing
   and 2 cups steamed broccoli
   and 2 large multigrain rice cakes
   or:
   4 oz. waterpack tuna on 4 cups greens + 2 tbsp. lowfat dressing
   with 1 cup fresh diced tomatoes
   and 1 cup cucumbers
   and ½ cup cooked black beans

PM Snack: 1 protein snack + 1 fruit
   Examples:
   1 oz. stick mozzarella cheese
   and 1 apple

Dinner: 1 protein + 2 vegetables + salad + 1 starch/grain + 1 extra
   Examples:
   6 oz. grilled lean beef
   and 1 cup steamed spinach + 1 cup steamed carrots
   and mixed green salad + 2 tbsp. lowfat dressing
   and ½ cup sweet potato or ½ cup brown rice
   and 1 cup grapes

*See "Extras" in Appendix A, page 150, for food items.

1,800-CALORIE MEAL PLAN

Protein	Fruit	Vegetable	Starch/Grain	Protein Snack	Extras*
4	3	4	4	2	3

Breakfast: 1 protein + 1 starch + 1 extra
Examples:
7 egg whites (hard boiled or omelet cooked with pan spray)
with 1/2 grapefruit and 1 slice whole grain toast + 1 tbsp. jam
or:
1 cup nonfat cottage cheese, 1 cup pineapple, and 1 English muffin
+ 1 tbsp. honey

Lunch: 1 protein + 2 vegetables + salad + 1 starch/grain + 1 extra
Examples:
3 oz. roasted chicken breast
with 4 cups of salad greens + 2 tbsp of lowfat dressing
and 2 cups steamed broccoli
and 2 large multigrain rice cakes
or:
4 oz. waterpack tuna on 4 cups greens + 2 tbsp. lowfat dressing
with 1 cup fresh diced tomatoes
and 1 cup cucumbers
and ½ cup cooked black beans

PM Snack: 1 protein snack + 1 fruit
Examples:
1 oz. stick mozzarella cheese
and 1 apple

Dinner: 1 protein + 2 vegetables + salad + 1 starch/grain + 1 extra
Examples:
6 oz. grilled lean beef
and 1 cup steamed spinach + 1 cup steamed carrots
and mixed green salad + 2 tbsp lowfat dressing
and ½ cup sweet potato or 1 cup steamed brown rice
and 1 cup grapes

*See "Extras" in Appendix A, page 150, for food items.

BIBLIOGRAPHY

"A History of Nutrition," EV McCollum 1957 QU 145 McCol.

Agus MSD, Swain JF, Larson CL, Eckert EA, Ludwig DS. (2000). Dietary composition and physiologic adaptations to energy restriction. Am J Clin Nutr 271, 901–07.

Ashley JM, St Jeor ST, Perumean-Chaney S, Schrage J, Bovee V. "Meal replacements in weight intervention." Obes Res. 2001 Nov;9 Suppl 4:312S–20S

Barr SI, Murphy SP, Agurs-Collins TD, Poos MI. (2003). Planning Diets for Individuals Using the Dietary Reference Intakes. Nutr Rev 61, 352–60.

Barringer TA, Kirk JK, Santaniello AC, Foley KL, Michielutte R. "Effect of a multivitamin and mineral supplement on infection and quality of life. A randomized, double-blind, placebo-controlled trial." Ann Intern Med. 2003;138(5):365–71.

Berdanier C, (2000). Proteins. In: "Advanced Nutrition: Macronutrients 2nd edition" pp. 130–96. CRC Press, Boca Raton.

Blot WJ, Li J-Y, Taylor PR, Guo W, Dawsey S, Wang G-Q, Yang CS, Zheng S-F, Gail M, Li G-Y, Yu Y, Liu B-Q, Tangrea J, Sun Y-H, Liu F, Fraumeni JF, Zhang Y-H, Li B. (1993).

Brand-Miller JC, Holt SH, Pawlak DB, McMillan J. (2002). Glycemic index and obesity. Am J Clin Nutr 76,281S–85S.

Callahan HS, Meeuws KE, Burden VR, Purnell JQ. A high-protein diet induces sustained reductions in appetite, ad libitum caloric intake, and body weight despite compensatory changes in diurnal plasma leptin and ghrelin concentrationsAm J Clin Nutr. 2005 Jul;82(1):41–8.

Calle EE, Thun MJ, (2004). Obesity and Cancer. Oncogene 23, 6365–78.

Campbell WW, Crim MC, Dallal GE, Young VR, Evans WJ. (1994). Increased protein requirements in elderly people: new data and retrospective reassessments. Am J ClinNutr 60, 501–09.

Cardiovascular Diseases Group. Cancer Information and Epidemiology Division, National Cancer Center Research Institute, Tokyo, Japan, J Natl Cancer Inst 9 5, 906–913.

Chandra RK, "Effect of vitamin and trace-element supplementation on immune responses and infection in elderly subjects." Lancet. 1992; 340: 1124–27.

Clarkson TB, Anthony MS, Morg an TM. Inhibition of postmenopausal atherosclerosis progression: a comparison of the effects of conjugated equine estrogens and soy phytoestrogens. J Clin Endocrinol Metab. 2001;86: 41–7.

Committee on Diet and Health. (1989). Diet and health: protein. In "Diet and Health: Implications for Reducing Chronic Disease Risk" pp. 259271. National Research Council, Food and Nutrition Board, Washington DC.

Dumesnil JG, Turgeon J, Tremblay A, Poirier P, Gilbert M, Gagnon L, St-Pierre S, Garneau C, Lemieux I, Pascot A, Bergeron J, Despres JP. (2001). Effect of a low-glycaemic index—lowfat—high protein diet on the atherogenic metabolic risk profile of abdominally obese men. Br J Nutr 86,557–68.

Ebbeling CB, Leidig MM, Sinclair KB, Hangen JP, Ludwig DS. (2003). A reduced-glycemic load diet in the treatment of adolescent obesity. Arch Pediatr Adolesc Med 1 5 7, 773–79.

Eisenstein J, Roberts SB, Dallal G, Saltzman E. (2002). High protein weight loss diets: are they safe and do they work? A review of experimental and epidemiologic data. Nutr Rev 60,189–200.

Epstein LH, Gordy CC, Raynor HA, Beddome M, Kilanowski CK, Paluch R. (2001). Increasing fruit and vegetable intake and decreasing fat and sugar intake in families at risk for childhood obesity. Obes Res 9,171–78.

Febbraio MA, Keenan J, Angus DJ, Campbell SE, Garnham AP. (2000). Pre-exercise carbohydrate ingestion, glucose kinetics, and muscle glycogen use: effect of the glycemic index. J Appl Physiol 89,1845–51.

Forbes GB, Welle SL. Lean body mass in obesity. Int J Obesity 1983; 7: 99–07.

Forbes GB. Lean body mass and fat in obese children. Pediatrics 1964; 34: 308–14.

Fuchs CS, Giovannucci EL, Colditz GA, Hunter DJ, Stampfer MJ, Rosner B, Speizer FE, Willett WC. (1999). Dietary fiber and the risk of colorectal cancer and adenoma in women. N Engl J Med 340, 169–76.

Fuller M, (2000). Proteins and amino acid requirements. In "Biochemical and Physiological Aspects of Human Nutrition" (M. Stipanuk, Ed), pp. 287–04. WB Saunders, Philadelphia.

Fung T, Hu FB, Fuchs C, Giovannucci E, Hunter DJ, Stampfer MJ, Colditz GA, Willett WC. (2003). Major dietary patterns and the risk of colorectal cancer in women. Arch Int Med 163,309–14.

Garza C, Scrimshaw NS, Young VR. (1977). Human protein requirements: a long-term metabolic nitrogen balance study in young men to evaluate the 1973 FAO/WHO safe level of egg protein intake. J Nutr 107, 335–52.

Gray DS. Changes in bioelectrical impedance during fasting. Am J Clin Nutr 1988; 48: 1184–1187.

Heber D, Bowerman S. (2001). What Color is Your Diet? Harper Collins, New York.

Hensrud DD "Dietary treatment and long-term weight loss and maintenance in type 2 diabetes." Obes Res. 2001 Nov;9 Suppl 4:348S-53S.

Heymsfield SB, van Mierlo CA, van der Knaap HC, Heo M, Frier HI. "Weight management us ing a meal replacement strategy: meta and pooling analysis from six studies." Int J Obes Relat Metab Disord. 2003 May;27(5):537–49.

Higginbotham S, Zhang ZF, Lee IM, Cook NR, Giovannucci E, Buring JE, Liu S. (2004). Dietary glycemic load and risk of colorectal cancer in the Women's Health Study. J Natl Canc Inst 96, 229–233.

Holmquist C, Larsson S, Wolk A de Faire U. "Multivitamin supplements are inversely associated with risk of myocardial infarction in men and women."—Stockholm Heart Epidemiology Program (SHEEP). J Nutr. 2003; 133: 2650–2654.

Howe JC, Rumpler WV, Behall KM. (1996). Dietary starch composition and level of energy intake alter nutrient oxidation in carbohydrate-sensitive men. J Nutr 1 2 6, 2120–29.

Jansen MC, Bueno-de-Mesquita HB, Buzina R, Fidanza F, Menotti A, Blackburn H, Nissinen AM, Kok FJ, K romhout D, Seven Countries Study Research Group. (1999). Dietary fiber and plant foods in relation to colorectal cancer mortality: the Seven Countries Study. Int J Cancer 8 1, 174–79.

Jenkins DJ, Wolever TM, Taylor RH, Barker H, Fielden H, Baldwin JM, Bowling AC, Newman HC, Jenkins AL, G off DV. (1981). Glycemic index of foods: a physiological basis for carbohydrate exchange. Am J Clin Nutr 34,362–66.

Johnston CS, Tjonn SL, Swan PD. (2004). High-protein, low-fat diets are effective for weight loss and favorably alter biomarkers in healthy adults. J Nutr 134, 586–91.

Karmali RA, Marsh J, Fuchs C. (1984). Effect of omega-3 fatty acids on growth of a rat mammary tumor. J Natl Cancer Inst 73,457–461.

Kim MH, Gutierrez AM, Goldfarb RH. (2002). Different mechanisms of soy isoflavones in cell cycle regulation and inhibition of invasion. Anticancer Res. 2 2, 3811–17.

Kreutler P, Czajka-Narins D. (1987). Protein. In: "Nutrition in Perspective" p. 121–162. Prentice Hall, Upper Saddle River.

Kris-Etherton PM, Lefevre M, Beecher R, Gross MD, Keen CL, Etherton TD, (2004). Bioactive compounds in nutrition and health-research methodologies for establishing biological function: the antioxidant and anti-inflammatory effects of flavonoids on atheros clerosis. Ann Rev Nutr 24,511–38.

Kushi LH, Folsom AR, Prineas RJ, Mink PJ, Wu Y et al. "Dietary antioxidant vitamins and death from coronary heart disease in postmenopausal women." N Engl JMed. 1996; 334(18_): 1156–62.

Layman DK, Boileau RA, Erickson DJ, Painter JE, Shiue H, Sather C, Christou DD. (2003). Reduced ratio of dietary carbohydrate to protein improves body composition and blood lipid profiles during weight loss in adult women. J Nutr 133, 411–17.

Ledikewe JH, Smiciklas-Wright H, Mitchell DC, Miller CK, Jensen GL. (2004). Dietary patterns of rural older adults are associated with weight and nutritional status. J Am Geriatr Soc 5 2, 589–95.

Lindner MA. (1991). A fish oil diet inhibits colon cancer in mice. Nutr Cancer 1 5, 1–11.

Liu S, Manson JE, Buring JE, Stampfer MJ, Willett WC, Ridker PM. (2002). Relation between a diet with a high glycemic load and plasma concentrations of high-sensitivity Creactive protein in middle-aged women. Am J Clin Nutr 75, 492–98.

Liu S. (1998). Dietary glycemic load, carbohydrate and whole grain intakes in relation to risk of coronary heart disease. Harvard University, Boston. 1998.

Lohman TG, Going SB, Golding L et al. Interlaboratory bioelectrical resistance comparison. Med Sci Sports Exerc 1987; 19: 539–45.

London SJ, Sacks FM, Caesar J, Stampfer MJ, Siguel E, Willett WC. (1991). Fatty acid composition of subcutaneous adipose tissue and diet in postmenopausal US women. Am J Clin Nutr 5 4, 340–45.

Ludwig DS, Majzoub JA, Al-Zahrani A, Dallal GE, Blanco I, Roberts SB. (1999). High glycemic index foods, overeating, and obesity. Pediatrics 103 : E26.

Ludwig DS. (2002). The glycemic index: physiological mechanisms relating to obesity, diabetes, and cardiovascular disease. JAMA 287, 2414–23.

Martínez ME, Marshall JR, Alberts DS, (1999). Dietary fiber, carbohydrates, and cancer. In "Nutritional Oncology," (D. Heber, G.L. Blackburn and V. L.W. Go, Eds), pp. 185–94. Academic Press, San Diego.

Matthews D. (1999). Proteins and amino acids. In "Modern Nutrition in Health and Disease, 9th ed." (Shils M, Olson J, Shike M, et al., eds.) pp. 11–48. Williams & Wilkins, Baltimore.

Mattisson I, Wirfalt E, Johansson U, Gullberg B, Olsson H, Berglund G. (2004). Intakes of plant foods, fibre and fat and risk of breast cancer—a prospective study in the Malmo Diet and Cancer cohort. Br J Cancer 9 0, 122–27.

McCullough ML, Giovannucci EL. (2004). Diet and cancer prevention. Oncogene 2 3, 6349–64.

McCullough ML, Robertson AS, Chao A, Jacobs EJ, Stampfer MJ, Jacobs DR, Diver WR, Calle EE, Thun MJ. (2003). A prospective study of whole grains, fruits, vegetables and colon cancer risk. Cancer Causes Control 1 4, 959–70.

McDowell M, Briefel R, Alaimo K, et al. (1994). Energy and macronutrient intakes of persons ages 2 months and over in the United States: Third National Health and Nutrition Examination Survey, Phase 1, 1988–91. US Government Printing Office, Vital and Health Statistics, Washington, DC.

Messina MJ, Persky V, Setchell KD, Barnes S. (1994). Soy intake and cancer risk: a review of the in vitro and in vivo data. Nutr Cancer 21, 113–31

Milner, J. (2002). Strategies for cancer prevention: the role of diet. Br J Nutr 8 7, S265–72.

MRC Vitamin Study Research Group. "Prevention of neural tube defects: results of the Medical Research Council Vitamin Study." Lancet. 1991; 338(8760): 131–7

National Research Council, Food and Nutrition Board. (1989). Recommended Dietary Allowances. 10th ed. National Academy Press, Washington, DC.

Nationwide Food Consumption Survey: Nutrient Intakes: Individuals in 48 States. Hyattsville, Md: US Dept of Agriculture, Consumer Nutrition Division, HNIS; 1977–78. Report No. 1-2.

Nutrition intervention trials in Linxiang, China: supplementation with specific vitamin/mineral combinations, cancer incidence, and disease-specific mortality in the general population. JNat Cancer Inst 85,1483–92.

Nutrition; An Integrated Approach, Ruth Pike and Myrtle Brown, John Wiley & Sons, 1975, pp 4–8.

Okuyama H, Kobayashi T, Watanbe S. (1996). Dietary fatty acids—the n-6/n-3 balance and chronic elderly diseases. Excess linoleic acid and relative n-3 deficiency syndrome seen in Japan. Prog Lipid Res 35, 409–57.

Osganian SK, Stampfer MJ, Rimm E, Spiegelman D, Hu FB, Manson JE, Willett WC. "Vitamin C and risk of coronary heart disease in women." JAm Coll Cardiol. 2003;42(2):246–52.

Perez CE. (2002). Fruit and vegetable consumption. Health Rep 1 3, 23–31.

Peterson G, Barnes S. (1996). Genistein inhibits both estrogen and growth factor-stimulated proliferation of human breast cancer cells. Cell Growth Differ 7, 1345–51.

Putnam JJ, Allshouse JA. (1999). Food consumption, prices, and expenditures, 1970–97. USDA, Washington DC.

Quatromoni PA, Copenhafer DL, D'Agostino RB, Millen BE. (2002). Dietary patterns predict thedevelopment of overweight in women: The Framingham Nutrition Studies. J Amer Diet Assoc 102, 1240–46.

Rohan TE, Howe GR, Friedenreich CM, Jain M, Miller AB. (1993). Dietary fiber, vitamins A, C, and E, and risk of breast cancer: a cohort study. Cancer Causes Control 4, 29–37.

Rose DP, Connolly JM, Meschter CL. (1991). Effect of dietary fat on human breast cancer growth and lung metastasis in nude mice. J Natl Cancer Inst 8 3, 1491–95.

Rose DP, Connolly JM. (1999). Omega-3 fatty acids as cancer chemopreventive agents. Pharmacol Ther 8 3, 217–244.

Rosen ED, Spiegelman BM. (2001). PPARgamma : a nuclear regulator of metabolism, differentiation, and cell growth. J Biol Chem 2 7 6, 37731–34.

Salmeron J, Ascherio A, Rimm EB, Colditz GA, Spiegelman D, Jenkins DJ, Stampfer MJ, Wing AL, Willett WC. (1997a). Dietary fiber, glycemic load, and risk of NIDDM in men. Diabetes Care 2 0, 545–50

Salmeron J, Manson JE, Stampfer MJ, Colditz GA, Wing AL, Willett WC. (1997b) Dietary fiber, glycemic load, and risk of non-insulin-dependent diabetes mellitus in women. JAMA 277, 472–77.

Schatzkin A, Lanza . Polyp Prevention Trial Study Group. (2002). Polyps and vegetables (and fat, fibre): the polyp prevention trial. IARC Sci Publ 156, 463–66.

Segal KR, Van Loan M, Fitzgerald PI, Hodgson JA, Van Italie, TB. Lean body mass estimation by bioelectrical impedance analysis: a four-site clinical validation study. Am J Clin Nutr 1988; 47: 7–14.

Simopoulos AP. (2001). N-3 fatty acids and human health: Defining strategies for public policy. Lipids 36:S83–89.

Skov AR, To u b ro S, Ronn B, Holm L, Astrup A. (1999). Randomized trial on protein vs carbohydrate in ad libitum fat reduced diet for the treatment of obesity. Int J Obes Related Metab Disord 23, 528–36.

Slabber M, Barnard HC, Kuyl JM, Dannhauser A, Schall R. (1994). Effects of a low-insulin-response, energy-restricted diet on weight loss and plasma insulin concentrations in hyperinsulinemic obese females. Am J Clin Nutr 60, 48–53.

Stampfer M, Hennekens C, Manson J, Colditz G, Rosner B et al. "Vitamin E consumption and the risk of coronary artery disease in women." N. Eng J Med. 1993; 328(20):1444–49.

Steinmetz KA, Potter JD. (1991). Vegetables, fruits, and cancer. I.Epidemiology. Cancer Causes and Control 2: 325–37.

Steinmetz KA, Potter JD. (1996). Vegetables, fruits and cancer prevention: a review. J Am Diet Assn. 10, 1027–39.

Stephens NG, Parsons A, Schofield PM, Kelly F, Cheeseman K et al. "Randomised controlled trial of vitamin E in patients with coronary disease: Cambridge Heart Antioxidant Study (CHAOS)." Lancet.1996; 347(9004): 781–86.

Swinburn BA, Caterson I, Seidell JC, James WP. (2004). Diet, nutrition and the prevention of excess weight gain and obesity. Public Health Nutr 7, 123–46.

Tarnopolsky M. (2004). Protein requirements for endurance athletes. Nutrition. 20, 662–68.

Tarnopolsky MA, Atkinson SA, MacDougall JD, Chesley A, Phillips S, Schwarcz HP. (1992). Evaluation of protein requirements for trained strength athletes. J Appl Physiol. 7 3, 1986–95.

Temple NJ. (2000). Antioxidants and disease: more questions than answers. Nutr Res 20, 449–59.

Tohill BC, Seymour J, Serdula M, Kettel-Khan L, Rolls BJ. (2004). What epidemiologic studies tell us about the relationship between fruit and vegetable consumption and body weight. Nutr Rev. 6 2, 365–74.

Tsai WS, Nagawa H, Kaizaki S, Tsuruo T, Muto T. (1998). Inhibitory effects of n–3 polyunsaturated fatty acids on sigmoid colon cancer transformants. J Gastroenterol 3 3, 206–12.

Verhoeven DT, Assen N, Goldbohm RA, Dorant E, van 't Veer P, Sturmans F, Hermus RJ, van den Brandt PA. (1997). Vitamins C and E, retinol, beta-carotene and dietary fiber in relation to breast cancer risk: a prospective cohort study. Br J Cancer 75, 149–55.

Way JM, Harrington WW, Brown KK, Gottschalk WK, Sundseth SS, Mansfield TA, Ramachandran RK, Willson TM, Kliewer SA. (2001). Comprehensive messenger ribonucleic acid profiling reveals that peroxisome proliferator-activated receptor gamma activation has coordinate effects on gene expression in multiple insulinsensitive tissues. Endocrinology 142, 1269–77.

Westerterp-Plantenga MS, Lejeune MP, Nihs I, van Ooijen M, Kovacs EM. (2004). High protein intake sustains weight maintenance after body weight loss in humans. Int J Obes Relat Metab Disord 2 8, 57–64.

Westerterp-Plantenga MS, Rolland V, Wilson SAJ, Westerterp KR. (1999). Satiety related to 24 h diet-induced thermogenesis during high protein/carbohydrate vs. high fat diets measured in a respiration chamber. Eur J Clin Nutr 53, 495–502.

Webster JD, Hesp R, Garrow JS. The composition of excess weight in obese women estimated by body density, total body water, and total body potassium. Human Nutrition: Clinical Nutrition 1984; 38C: 299–06.

Weigle DS, Breen PA, Matthys CC, Willett WC, Hunter DJ, Stampfer MJ, Colditz G, Manson JE, Spiegelman D, Rosner B, Hennekens CH, Speizer FE. (1992). Dietary fat and fiber in relation to risk of breast cancer: an 8-year follow-up. J Am Med Assoc 2 6 8, 2037–44.

Willett WC. (1994). Diet and health: what should we eat? Science 2 5 4, 532–37.

Willett WC. (1995). Diet, nutrition and avoidable cancer. Environ Health Perspect 103, 165–71.

Willson TM, Brown PJ, Sternbach DD Henke BR. (2000). The PPARs: From Orphan Receptors to Drug Discovery. J Med Chem 4 3, 527–50.

Woɪfrum C, Borrmann, CM, Borchers T, Spener F. (2001). Fatty acids and hypolipidemic drugs regulate receptors alpha—and gamma-mediated gene expression via liver fatty acid binding protein: a signaling path to the nucleus. Proc. Natl. Acad. Sci. U.S.A. 98, 23.

World Cancer Research Fund. (1997). Food, Nutrition and the Prevention of Cancer: A Global Perspective. American Institute for Cancer Research, Washington, DC.

Yamamoto S, Sobue T, Kobayashi M, Sasaki S, Tsugane S. S(2003). Soy, isoflavones, and breast cancer risk in Japan. Japan Public Health Center-Based Prospective Study on Cancer

Yang M-U. Body composition and resting metabolic rate in obesity. In: Obesity and Weight Control (Frankle RT and Yang M-U, eds.) Aspen Publishers, Rockville , 1988 pp.71–96.

Zhang X, Shu XO, Gao YT, Yang G, Li Q, Li H, Jin F, Zheng W. (2003). Soy food consumption is associated with a lower risk of coronary heart disease in Chinese women. J Nutr 133, 2874–78.

INDEX